# TRANSACTIONAL LAWYERING SKILLS

EDITORIAL ADVISORS

**Vicki Been**
Elihu Root Professor of Law
New York University School of Law

**Erwin Chemerinsky**
Dean and Distinguished Professor of Law
University of California, Irvine, School of Law

**Richard A. Epstein**
Laurence A. Tisch Professor of Law
New York University School of Law
Peter and Kirsten Bedford Senior Fellow
The Hoover Institution
Senior Lecturer in Law
The University of Chicago

**Ronald J. Gilson**
Charles J. Meyers Professor of Law and Business
Stanford University
Marc and Eva Stern Professor of Law and Business
Columbia Law School

**James E. Krier**
Earl Warren DeLano Professor of Law
The University of Michigan Law School

**Richard K. Neumann, Jr.**
Professor of Law
Hofstra University School of Law

**Robert H. Sitkoff**
John L. Gray Professor of Law
Harvard Law School

**David Alan Sklansky**
Yosef Osheawich Professor of Law
University of California at Berkeley School of Law

**Kent D. Syverud**
Dean and Ethan A. H. Shepley University Professor
Washington University School of Law

**Elizabeth Warren**
Leo Gottlieb Professor of Law
Harvard Law School

ASPEN COURSEBOOK SERIES

# TRANSACTIONAL LAWYERING SKILLS

**Client Interviewing, Counseling, and Negotiation**

**RICHARD K. NEUMANN, JR.**
Maurice A. Deane School of Law at
Hofstra University

**Wolters Kluwer**
Law & Business

Copyright © 2013 Richard K. Neumann, Jr.

Published by Wolters Kluwer Law & Business in New York.

Wolters Kluwer Law & Business serves customers worldwide with CCH, Aspen Publishers, and Kluwer Law International products. (www.wolterskluwerlb.com)

No part of this publication may be reproduced or transmitted in any form or by any means, electronic or mechanical, including photocopy, recording, or utilized by any information storage or retrieval system, without written permission from the publisher. For information about permissions or to request permissions online, visit us at www.wolterskluwerlb.com, or a written request may be faxed to our permissions department at 212-771-0803.

To contact Customer Service, e-mail customer.service@wolterskluwer.com, call 1-800-234-1660, fax 1-800-901-9075, or mail correspondence to:

> Wolters Kluwer Law & Business
> Attn: Order Department
> PO Box 990
> Frederick, MD 21705

Printed in the United States of America.

4 5 6 7 8 9 0

ISBN 978-1-4548-2232-5

Library of Congress Cataloging-in-Publication Data

Neumann, Richard K., 1947-
  Transactional lawyering skills : client interviewing, counseling, and negotiation / Richard K. Neumann.
      p. cm.
  Includes bibliographical references.
  ISBN 978-1-4548-2232-5
  1. Practice of law—United States. I. Title.
KF300.N48 2012
340'.14—dc23
                                                                          2012038983

# About Wolters Kluwer Law & Business

Wolters Kluwer Law & Business is a leading global provider of intelligent information and digital solutions for legal and business professionals in key specialty areas, and respected educational resources for professors and law students. Wolters Kluwer Law & Business connects legal and business professionals as well as those in the education market with timely, specialized authoritative content and information-enabled solutions to support success through productivity, accuracy and mobility.

Serving customers worldwide, Wolters Kluwer Law & Business products include those under the Aspen Publishers, CCH, Kluwer Law International, Loislaw, Best Case, ftwilliam.com and MediRegs family of products.

**CCH** products have been a trusted resource since 1913, and are highly regarded resources for legal, securities, antitrust and trade regulation, government contracting, banking, pension, payroll, employment and labor, and healthcare reimbursement and compliance professionals.

**Aspen Publishers** products provide essential information to attorneys, business professionals and law students. Written by preeminent authorities, the product line offers analytical and practical information in a range of specialty practice areas from securities law and intellectual property to mergers and acquisitions and pension/benefits. Aspen's trusted legal education resources provide professors and students with high-quality, up-to-date and effective resources for successful instruction and study in all areas of the law.

**Kluwer Law International** products provide the global business community with reliable international legal information in English. Legal practitioners, corporate counsel and business executives around the world rely on Kluwer Law journals, looseleafs, books, and electronic products for comprehensive information in many areas of international legal practice.

**Loislaw** is a comprehensive online legal research product providing legal content to law firm practitioners of various specializations. Loislaw provides attorneys with the ability to quickly and efficiently find the necessary legal information they need, when and where they need it, by facilitating access to primary law as well as state-specific law, records, forms and treatises.

**Best Case Solutions** is the leading bankruptcy software product to the bankruptcy industry. It provides software and workflow tools to flawlessly streamline petition preparation and the electronic filing process, while timely incorporating ever-changing court requirements.

**ftwilliam.com** offers employee benefits professionals the highest quality plan documents (retirement, welfare and non-qualified) and government forms (5500/PBGC, 1099 and IRS) software at highly competitive prices.

**MediRegs** products provide integrated health care compliance content and software solutions for professionals in healthcare, higher education and life sciences, including professionals in accounting, law and consulting.

Wolters Kluwer Law & Business, a division of Wolters Kluwer, is headquartered in New York. Wolters Kluwer is a market-leading global information services company focused on professionals.

To the memory of my uncle John R. Benedict, Sr.
and for my aunt Marilyn Benedict together with
Rocky, Carl, Linda, Laura, and their families

# SUMMARY OF CONTENTS

*Contents* xi
*Preface* xv
*Acknowledgments* xvii

Chapter 1   Transactional Lawyering   1

## PART I   BECOMING A LAWYER   7

Chapter 2   Becoming a Professional   9
Chapter 3   Problem-Solving and Problem-Prevention   15
Chapter 4   Oral Communication Skills   27

## PART II   WORKING WITH TRANSACTIONAL CLIENTS   35

Chapter 5   Lawyering for and with Clients   37
Chapter 6   Interviewing Transactional Clients   43

## PART III   TRANSACTIONAL COUNSELING AND ADVISING   51

Chapter 7    Counseling and Advising Transactional Clients   53
Chapter 8    Some Examples of Counseling and Advice   59
Chapter 9    Preparing for Counseling: Developing Options   67
Chapter 10   Counseling Conversations with Transactional Clients   73
Chapter 11   Some Common Problems in Counseling   79

## PART IV   TRANSACTIONAL NEGOTIATION   87

Chapter 12   Negotiation by Lawyers in Transactions   89
Chapter 13   Interests, Rights, and Power   97
Chapter 14   Problem-Solving and Positional Approaches—Collegial and Combative Styles   103
Chapter 15   Negotiation Discussions with the Other Party's Lawyer   109
Chapter 16   Some Common Problems in Negotiation   119

## APPENDICES 125

Appendix A  Types of Contracts  127
Appendix B  Document Design for Contracts  131
Appendix C  Some Contract Drafting Considerations  135
Appendix D  Contract Conditions  139
Appendix E  Managing the Risk of the Unknown: Due Diligence, Representations, and Warranties  143

*Index*  149

# CONTENTS

*Preface xv*
*Acknowledgments xvii*

**Chapter 1  Transactional Lawyering  1**

§1.1  How the Book Is Organized  1
§1.2  Representing Clients in Disputes Is Only Part of What Lawyers Do—The Rest Is Transactional  1
§1.3  All Transactions Have Deal Stages, but Only Some Have Dispute Stages  2
§1.4  Business Issues and Legal Issues  3
§1.5  Different Types of Deals and Different Degrees of Lawyer Involvement  4

## PART I  BECOMING A LAWYER  7

**Chapter 2  Becoming a Professional  9**

§2.1  Excellent Judgment and Integrity Are a Lawyer's Two Most Valuable Assets  9
§2.2  Effective Lawyers Solve or Prevent Problems While Working Toward Specific Goals  10
§2.3  Assumptions Can Sabotage Good Lawyering  10
§2.4  Preparation, Efficiency, and Good Oral Communication Are Essential  11
§2.5  Numbers Matter—and So Do Taxes  12
§2.6  Overlawyering Can Be as Harmful as Underlawyering  13
§2.7  Professionalism Is a Way of Being  14

**Chapter 3  Problem-Solving and Problem-Prevention  15**

§3.1  Diagnosis, Prediction, and Strategy in Professional Work  15
§3.2  How Professionals Diagnose, Predict, and Strategize  17
§3.3  Thinking Divergently as Well as Convergently  20

xii    Contents

    §3.4 Developing a Problem-Solving Style 21
    §3.5 The Inclusive Solution 24

**Chapter 4** **Oral Communication Skills** **27**

    §4.1 Listening and—More Important Hearing 27
    §4.2 Active Listening 29
    §4.3 Asking Questions 30
    §4.4 Communicating Empathy 32
    §4.5 Painting a Picture 33
    §4.6 Using Tone of Voice and Body Language 33
    §4.7 Making Arguments 34

## PART II WORKING WITH TRANSACTIONAL CLIENTS 35

**Chapter 5** **Lawyering For and With Clients** **37**

    §5.1 Client-Centered Lawyering 37
    §5.2 The Client as a Colleague and Collaborator 38
    §5.3 Who Decides What 40
    §5.4 What Clients Like and Dislike in a Lawyer 41
    §5.5 Working with Transactional Clients 42

**Chapter 6** **Interviewing Transactional Clients** **43**

    §6.1 Types of Client Interviews 43
    §6.2 Short-Conversation Client Interviewing 44
    §6.3 Long-Conversation Client Interviewing 44
    §6.4 Organizing the Long-Conversation Interview 45
    §6.5 Preparing for the Long-Conversation Interview 45
    §6.6 Beginning the Interview 46
    §6.7 What to Ask About 47
    §6.8 Sequencing and Formulating Questions 49
    §6.9 Ending 50

## PART III COUNSELING AND ADVICE 51

**Chapter 7** **Counseling and Advising Transactional Clients** **53**

    §7.1 The Difference Between Counseling and Advice 53
    §7.2 "Decision-making Is an Art" 54
    §7.3 Four Challenges in Counseling 55
    §7.4 Why Some Clients Exclude Their Lawyers from Important Decisions 55

**Chapter 8** **Some Examples of Counseling and Advice** **59**

    §8.1 Advice 59
    §8.2 Counseling 60

| | | |
|---|---|---|
| | §8.3 | Counseling on a Very Large Scale (The Plant Closing) 61 |
| | | §8.3.1 Preparing to Counsel the Employees 61 |
| | | §8.3.2 Meeting with the Steering Committee 65 |
| **Chapter 9** | **Preparing for Counseling: Structuring the Options 67** | |
| | §9.1 | Focusing on Client Goals and Preferences 67 |
| | §9.2 | Developing Options (Potential Solutions) 68 |
| | §9.3 | Predicting What Each Option Would Cause 68 |
| | §9.4 | Adapting to the Client's Tolerance for Risk 70 |
| **Chapter 10** | **Counseling Conversations with Transactional Clients 73** | |
| | §10.1 | Mood, Setting, and the Lawyer's Affect 73 |
| | §10.2 | Beginning the Discussion 75 |
| | §10.3 | Discussing the Choices and What They Would Do 76 |
| | §10.4 | If the Client Asks for a Recommendation, Should You Give One? 76 |
| | §10.5 | Asking the Client to Decide 78 |
| **Chapter 11** | **Some Common Problems in Counseling and Advice 79** | |
| | §11.1 | Ethical Issues in Counseling 79 |
| | §11.2 | When the Lawyer Suspects That the Client's Stated Goal Might Not Really Be What the Client Wants 81 |
| | §11.3 | When the Client Makes a Decision the Lawyer Considers Extremely Unwise 83 |
| | §11.4 | When the Client Has Been Persuaded by Cognitive Illusions 83 |
| | §11.5 | Guarding Against Your Own Cognitive Illusions 85 |

## PART IV  TRANSACTIONAL NEGOTIATION  87

| | | |
|---|---|---|
| **Chapter 12** | **Negotiation by Lawyers in Transactions 89** | |
| | §12.1 | The Two Negotiations—Business Issues and Legal Issues 89 |
| | §12.2 | What to Negotiate—The Legal Issues 91 |
| | §12.3 | Much of Legal-Issue Negotiation Is Really About Labels 93 |
| | §12.4 | Preparing to Negotiate 94 |
| | §12.5 | Working with the Client During the Negotiation 95 |
| **Chapter 13** | **Interests, Rights, and Power 97** | |
| | §13.1 | Each Party's Interests 97 |
| | §13.2 | Each Party's Rights 98 |

§13.3 Each Party's Power 99
§13.4 Best Alternative to a Negotiated Agreement (BATNA) 100

**Chapter 14 Problem-Solving and Positional Approaches—Collegial and Combative Styles 103**

§14.1 Problem-Solving vs. Positional Negotiation 103
§14.2 The Problem-Solving Approach 103
§14.3 The Positional Approach 105
§14.4 What to Do When the Other Side Refuses to Problem-Solve 106
§14.5 Negotiating Styles—Collegial and Combative 106
§14.6 An Example of Style 107

**Chapter 15 Negotiation Discussions with the Other Party's Lawyer 109**

§15.1 Telephone, Email, Location 109
§15.2 Planning the Issues Agenda 111
§15.3 Requests, Demands, Offers, and Concessions 112
§15.4 Who Drafts 116
§15.5 Information Bargaining 117

**Chapter 16 Some Common Problems in Negotiation 119**

§16.1 Ethical Issues in Negotiation 119
§16.2 Threats and Warnings 121

# APPENDICES 125

**Appendix A** Types of Contracts 127
**Appendix B** Document Design for Contracts 131
**Appendix C** Some Contract Drafting Considerations 135
**Appendix D** Contract Conditions 139
**Appendix E** Managing the Risk of the Unknown: Due Diligence, Representations, and Warranties 143

*Index* 149

# PREFACE

Nearly all skills books explain what litigators do. This one instead explains what transactional lawyers, or more specifically deal lawyers, do — how they solve and prevent problems; how they interview, counsel, and advise clients; and how they negotiate. (It's not, however, a drafting textbook.)

In a contract drafting course, the book supplements a drafting textbook to explain the skills that surround contract drafting. While learning how to draft contracts, students can also learn how to negotiate a contract's legal issues and how to advise and counsel clients about contract problems.

Parts of the book can also be used in the first-year Contracts course to provide a practical context for much of what students read in casebooks. It can be valuable where some skills coverage is being added to a doctrinal course. The book explains, for example, how and why lawyers negotiate conditions, representations, and warranties. With those explanations and with others, skills exercises can be inserted at strategic points in the course.

I teach an upper-division contract drafting course, called Transactional Lawyering, as well as the first-year Contracts course. In the contract drafting course, I use the entire book. In first-year Contracts, I use selected materials from the book.

The book can also be useful in courses that cover a particular market or industry, such as commercial leasing or entertainment law, where a skills component is being added.

Richard K. Neumann, Jr.
November 2012

# ACKNOWLEDGMENTS

I'm grateful to Tina Stark for teaching so many of us how contracts work and how to draft them; to Stef Krieger for generously allowing some of his negotiation material from *Essential Lawyering Skills* to appear in the negotiation chapters of this book; to Grace Hum, Lyn Entrikin, and Aspen's anonymous reviewers for many suggestions and helpful comments; to Carol McGeehan for suggesting the idea of this book; to Dana Wilson for providing, as always, excellent editorial guidance; to Ellen Littman for insights that informed the writing; to Elanie Cintron, Farihah Karim, George Pleasant-Jones, Michelle Chin Que, Lisa Brabant, Karen Nielson, and Frances Zemel for research assistance; and to Alex and Lill for everything else.

# TRANSACTIONAL LAWYERING SKILLS

# CHAPTER 1

# TRANSACTIONAL LAWYERING

## §1.1 HOW THE BOOK IS ORGANIZED

This book explains how lawyers interview and counsel transactional clients and negotiate on their behalf.

This chapter and Chapters 2 through 4 describe core concepts of transactional work and of the practice of law generally, including professionalism, problem-solving, problem-prevention, and oral communication skills. These chapters are a foundation for the rest of the book.

Chapters 5 and 6 introduce clients and transactional interviewing. Chapters 7 through 11 explain how lawyers counsel and advise clients in transactions, particularly in helping clients make important decisions.

Chapters 12 through 16 explain how lawyers negotiate in transactions. These chapters cover topics such as problem-solving versus positional negotiation, negotiation styles, and negotiation conversations.

To help with some of the skills covered in the chapters, the book's appendices explain several background concepts, including types of contracts, document design, contract conditions, due diligence, and representations and warranties.

This book does not teach contract drafting. Rather, it teaches the skills that surround drafting in the life of a transactional lawyer.

## §1.2 REPRESENTING CLIENTS IN DISPUTES IS ONLY PART OF WHAT LAWYERS DO—THE REST IS TRANSACTIONAL

Movies and television almost invariably show lawyers cross-examining witnesses and making arguments to judges and juries—in other words, litigating. And law is taught through cases, or, more precisely, through judicial opinions that resolve litigation. But many lawyers almost never go near a courtroom.

About half of what the legal profession does is transactional work: representing clients who want to accomplish a positive goal of some kind other than winning a dispute with an adversary. Very often the situation is contractual: two parties have agreed to do a trade with each other, and lawyers will turn their agreement into a contract. Other transactional work might not involve contracts. Will drafting is transactional. So is persuading a regulatory agency to approve something the client wants.

This book concentrates on contracts, however, and uses the word *transactional* mostly in that sense.

Some lawyers do only litigation. Some do only transactional work. And some do both.

Litigation lawyers and transactional lawyers approach legal problems differently and in some respects see the world differently. Litigators fight to protect clients who are already in conflict with somebody else. Transactional lawyers plan and draft documents to achieve the client's goals while minimizing the risk of future conflict. Litigators try to win through public performances in courtrooms and through motions and negotiation ancillary to the courtroom. Transactional lawyers work less dramatically and almost entirely in offices.

Litigation is what social scientists call a zero-sum game: what one side gains is what the other side loses, averaging out to zero. If a plaintiff gains a $100,000 verdict, the defendant loses $100,000. It's really more complicated than that, but one party's gain is usually another party's loss.

Transactional work, however, is usually not a zero-sum game. If two parties deal—agree to trade money for goods, services, intellectual property licenses, or other things of value—each of them anticipates becoming better off as a result. If the deal works as planned, it's a win-win situation. The deal lawyer's job is to plan, counsel, negotiate, and draft to increase the odds that the deal will work as the client had hoped.

## §1.3 ALL TRANSACTIONS HAVE DEAL STAGES, BUT ONLY A FEW HAVE DISPUTE STAGES

The deal stage is where the transaction is created. The parties agree that they'll do a trade, usually a trade of money for property, services, or something else. Transactional lawyers work at the deal stage, primarily on the legal issues with a degree of involvement appropriate to the type of transaction.

In nearly all transactions, the deal works out. Each party performs to the satisfaction of the other. Or, if one party is dissatisfied, the parties work out a solution themselves, without consulting lawyers. A retail appliance store, for example, calls up its wholesale supplier and complains that the supplier's deliveries have been late, costing the retailer to lose sales to consumers. The retailer mentions that it might start buying from competing suppliers that sell the same appliances. To avoid losing business to competitors, the supplier promises to do better in the future and offers a token appeasement, such as a discount on the retailer's next order. The retailer considers that fair. The conversation ends with pleasantries. Nobody thinks about consulting a lawyer.

The parties can do this because business people value their reputations for reliability. They don't want to be known for not keeping promises. And they value existing profitable relationships and don't want to lose business to competitors. Many business people, though not all of them, can also be persuaded to be fair. Lawyers are an expense, and parties bring them in only if the stakes are big enough to justify the cost.

In some transactions, things go bad; the parties can't work out the problem themselves; and the dollar-value of the issues are worth paying a lawyer, at least for dispute advice and perhaps for more. One party's lawyer might start by haggling with the other party's lawyer over the telephone. In most of these situations, the parties work out a solution with help from their lawyers. If they can't, the aggrieved party has to decide whether to swallow the loss or to sue.

Only a tiny proportion—a *very* tiny proportion—of transactions end up in lawsuits. Business people instinctively know that in litigation both parties usually lose something. They lose through lawyers' fees, employee downtime, reputational damage, anxiety, and uncertainty. Only if the plaintiff wins and gets substantial damages would that be a reasonable investment. The plaintiff's payoff might not come until years later, after discovery, motions, trial, appeal, and so on. Regardless of who wins in court, the defendant loses something because all those litigation costs don't buy improvement in the defendant's position. The most they can buy is preventing the plaintiff from winning.

At the deal stage, one of the responsibilities of a transactional lawyer is to draft the contract to reduce the odds of a dispute occurring later and to put the client in a better position to cope with disputes if they do occur. Part of a deal lawyer's job is to keep the client away from litigators by preventing problems.

Some lawyers do both transactional and dispute work. This is more common in small firms than in large ones. The larger the firm, the more likely it is for a lawyer to specialize either in deals or in litigation but not both. In large firms, transactional lawyers often call themselves deal lawyers, but a deal lawyer is any lawyer who represents a client at the deal stage.

## §1.4 BUSINESS ISSUES AND LEGAL ISSUES

In transactional work, the word *term* has three separate meanings. As elsewhere in life, it can mean a word or phrase ("the term 'informed consent' appears in several statutes"). Or it can mean a period of time ("a copyright license for a term of ten years"). Or it can mean a provision in a contract. This section of the book uses the third meaning.

An issue is something about which the parties have not yet agreed. After they reach agreement on that issue, it becomes a term. While the parties are haggling over delivery dates, for example, the delivery schedule is an issue. Once they agree on dates, the schedule they've agreed on becomes a term in the contract.

The business issues are what the parties are trading (goods in exchange for money, for example) and how they've decided to accomplish the trade (when and how the seller will deliver the goods, for example, and when and how the buyer will pay).

The legal issues are what lawyers can add to the trade. Will the seller represent and warrant that the goods have certain characteristics? If the buyer makes a tardy payment, what will be the consequences? If an avalanche prevents the seller from delivering the goods on time, will the seller be in breach? Will either party be forbidden to assign its rights or delegate its duties to someone else? May either party terminate the contract, and if so, under what circumstances and with what consequences?

## §1.5 DIFFERENT TYPES OF DEALS AND DIFFERENT DEGREES OF LAWYER INVOLVEMENT

Often parties do their deal (agree and then perform) with no help from a lawyer. For example, you stop at a gas station, go inside and pay with cash on the counter, return to the pump, fill your car's gas tank, and drive away. No lawyers are in sight.

If you had paid with a credit card, the payment aspect of the transaction would have been governed by at least two standard-form contracts, both drafted by lawyers. One is your contract with the bank that issued your credit card. Another is the contract between the gas station and the bank to which the gas station will submit the charge against your credit card account. You and the gas station owner will never meet those lawyers. The contracts they drafted are nonnegotiable.

The gas station is probably a franchisee of a large petroleum company. That company's lawyers drafted a standard-form franchise contract years ago. The company probably will not negotiate the legal terms in those contracts, but they might be willing to negotiate on business issues. The franchisee gas station owner should consult a lawyer before signing that contract, but the lawyer's role will be primarily to explain the contract to the owner rather than to negotiate any of its terms. The only issues that might be negotiated are the business terms, which the gas station owner can settle directly with the petroleum company. The company's lawyers might have no role other than the one they played years ago: drafting the standard-form contract.

If the petroleum company is being bought by and merged into another petroleum company, the two companies' executives will negotiate the business issues—and there will be many of them—in great detail. At some point, the deal will be turned over to each company's lawyers, who will negotiate the legal issues and memorialize all the terms, business and legal, into a contract. This is a lawyer-to-lawyer negotiated contract, one in which lawyers on both sides are dealing with each other. Because mergers that violate the antitrust laws can be enjoined in a lawsuit brought by the federal government, the lawyers might perform another function of a transactional lawyer: shepherding the deal through regulatory approval, in this instance by persuading the Antitrust Division of the Justice Department to approve the merger.

Sometimes a party will ask its lawyer to negotiate some of the business issues as well as the legal issyess. This can happen where the party is inexperienced at business and wants an experienced negotiator to act as the party's agent. A lawyer with good business experience is a natural choice. In fact, the earliest sports agents were lawyers for this reason. The first time athletes attempted to negotiate through an agent was in 1965, when two baseball pitchers, Sandy Koufax and Don Drysdale, brought in a lawyer after rejecting contracts offered by their team, the Los Angeles Dodgers. The lawyer played only a small part in that negotiation, but other lawyers later took on larger roles, and some of them became sports agents as part of their law practice.

Sometimes the business issues and legal issues are so intertwined that the parties will bring their lawyers into the negotiation to help work out the business issues. And a lawyer might volunteer advice on a business issue ("I've seen other buyers pay less lately, and you might be paying too much in this deal"). But generally a lawyer doesn't negotiate business terms unless specifically authorized to do so by her client.

# PART I

# BECOMING A LAWYER

# CHAPTER 2

# BECOMING A PROFESSIONAL

## §2.1 EXCELLENT JUDGMENT AND INTEGRITY ARE A LAWYER'S TWO MOST VALUABLE ASSETS

*Excellent Judgment:* Judgment is knowing what to do and say—and what not to do or say—to improve a situation or prevent it from getting worse. Professionals decide what to do, and excellent judgment is the single most important characteristic that separates good decision-making from bad decision-making. When clients rely on you, they are relying on your judgment more than anything else.

Knowledge of the law is not enough. A lawyer who knows the law but lacks good judgment is a lawyer who sounds well informed but makes too many avoidable mistakes.

Judgment is the ability to know what actions and words are most likely to solve problems or, ideally, prevent them. It depends on situation sense—an instinct for reading between the lines and figuring out what's really going on, without being told explicitly. It operates on several levels at once—the practical, the ethical, and the moral—and it includes "appreciating the hidden complexity in questions that seem easy when they are posed in the abstract."[1]

The phrase *a prudent lawyer* refers to one whose judgment can safely be relied upon. A prudent lawyer foresees risk, makes sure that mistakes don't happen, and, to the extent possible, keeps clients out of trouble.

---

1. David Luban & Michael Millemann, *Good Judgment: Ethics Teaching in Dark Times*, 9 Geo. J. Leg. Ethics 71 (1995).

*Integrity:* Integrity means an honesty so thorough that anyone who knows the lawyer trusts her; a sense for what's right and fair so reliable that others respect the lawyer's moral voice; and an understanding of appropriateness that prevents the lawyer from crossing over into questionable conduct. It includes a strong feeling of responsibility for the matters entrusted to the lawyer's care, the strength to resist pressure to do the wrong thing, and humility. A lawyer with integrity treats everyone with respect and empathy, regardless of their station in life.

A lawyer who's recognized for integrity is a lawyer who will be trusted instinctively by clients and other lawyers. That makes integrity a professional asset, but it also has a deeper value. If you know that you've acted with integrity, you can have greater confidence in and respect for yourself.

## §2.2 EFFECTIVE LAWYERS SOLVE OR PREVENT PROBLEMS WHILE WORKING TOWARD SPECIFIC GOALS

*Solving problems—or, ideally, preventing them:* Rather than practice law in the literal sense, an effective lawyer uses law as one of many tools to solve or prevent problems. Solving a problem is converting it into a nonproblem or at least reducing its harmful effects. Preventing a problem is foreseeing risk and proactively doing whatever is necessary to reduce its odds of becoming a problem. These skills are explained in Chapter 3.

Some transactional lawyers are so good at this that clients seek their advice on problems that have no legal issues. When a corporation puts one of its own lawyers on its board of directors, it's because the lawyer has become respected for problem-solving and problem-preventing skills *generally*, not just in law.

*Identifying specific goals and organizing work to accomplish them:* The client wants something, and that's the overall or ultimate goal. To achieve it, the lawyer must do a number of things along the way—work out the legal issues and draft contract language that makes a copyright licensing deal work; persuade the Antitrust Division of the Justice Department to allow the client's merger with a competitor; or figure out a legal basis on which ranchers and environmentalists can reconstrue their differences to find some interests in common. Effective lawyers know exactly what the goals are and focus their work on accomplishing them. They don't work aimlessly on whatever is in the client's file.

## §2.3 ASSUMPTIONS CAN SABOTAGE GOOD LAWYERING

Suppose you realize that you need to make a particular decision in the next day or so. You also realize that you need to know six things to make this decision. You already know five of them. You've made a guess about the sixth thing, and you're confident that your guess is accurate. You could rely on your guess (make an assumption), or you could devote some effort to finding out what the truth is.

When lawyers make assumptions, they and their clients can get hurt. That's because guesses often turn out to be wrong. It's also because clients hire lawyers for important matters, where mistakes can cause real harm.

Not all assumptions are bad. Sometimes a lawyer will properly make a *temporary* assumption because the truth can't be discovered right away and work must proceed in the meantime. Sometimes a lawyer will balance risks and make an assumption because the decision involved is small and the cost of learning the truth is larger than that. And sometimes a lawyer will be forced to make an assumption because the truth can't be learned.

But many of the assumptions you'll be tempted to make shouldn't be made. As a general rule, if you don't know whether something is true, find out, if reasonably feasible. And if you must make an assumption, do it explicitly so that you and the people who rely on you know what's happening.

The most dangerous assumptions are the *unconscious* ones—the ones you don't realize you're making. Suppose you're chatting with someone in a social situation. Some of the things the other person says are based on matters that you don't fully know. You might ask a few questions, but for the most part you assume underlying facts without even realizing that you're doing it. You make these assumptions unconsciously because you don't want to appear dumb. And you don't want to be a pest, constantly interrupting with fussy questions. Most of what we discuss socially isn't important enough to justify cross-examining everyone around us to make sure we're making no assumptions.

But in lawyering, an unconscious assumption can be dangerous. You can't control it because you don't realize you're making it. And you can't gauge the risk of assuming something rather than knowing. The only way to overcome this problem is to learn to recognize what you don't know and consciously decide what to do about what you don't know.

## §2.4 PREPARATION, EFFICIENCY, AND GOOD ORAL COMMUNICATION ARE ESSENTIAL

*Preparation:* "Winging it" is sloppy and dangerous lawyering. Many lawyering tasks are like icebergs: What the bystander sees (the tip of the iceberg or the visible part of the lawyer's performance) is a tiny fraction of what supports it (the undersea part of the iceberg or the preparation for the performance). In lawyering, the ratio of preparation to performance can easily reach 15 or 20 to 1. It might take 10 hours to prepare for a half-hour counseling session with a client, and it might take 15 hours to prepare for a negotiating meeting that lasts two hours.

In preparation, resourcefulness counts more than brilliance. Few legal problems are solved by astute insights that no one has thought of before. Most legal problems are solved by diligently learning the details that matter and putting them together into a package that gets results.

*Efficiency:* Efficiency is getting the best results from a unit of effort, such as a billable hour. It's a ratio between work and gain. A lawyer is more efficient than others if she gets more results from a billable hour or if she gets the same results in less than a billable hour.

The efficient lawyer prospers while the inefficient lawyer works hard without having much to show for it. Many business clients audit their own law firms' bills to figure out whether the lawyers have used the most cost-effective ways of solving problems. Law firms that fail this scrutiny lose clients. It's difficult to be efficient without working hard, but hard work isn't the same as efficiency. Many inefficient lawyers work long hours without serving their clients well—and they lose clients who figure that out.

Time—including other people's time—is a resource to be used efficiently. A 20-minute conversation with a partner or a client wastes everyone's time if it covers only five minutes of content. The client or partner will assume that the lawyer who has wasted his time uses her own time inefficiently in other respects as well. The client will think about that when deciding whether to pay all or only part of the lawyer's bill. The supervising partner will think about it when deciding whether the lawyer's salary is being used efficiently.

*Oral Communication:* Lawyers spend a very large amount of their time in conversation—with clients, clients' employees, and other lawyers. These conversations aren't like courtroom oral arguments. And they aren't like the Socratic dialogs in casebook classrooms. They require a separate group of skills, which are explained in Chapter 4.

## §2.5 NUMBERS MATTER—AND SO DO TAXES

*Numbers:* Much of what lawyers do involves the allocation of money and other quantifiable resources. Quantities require math. If in drafting a contract, you've expressed the math inaccurately or ambiguously, you may have created a lawsuit. The parties might sue each other, asking a court to decide what the math should have been. And your client might sue you for malpractice. Math can be power. In negotiation, if the other lawyer understands the numbers better than you do, you might agree to something that's not as good as you thought it would be, while the other lawyer smiles a secret smile.

*Taxes:* Whenever money changes hands, the transaction might have tax consequences. You cannot counsel or negotiate well without being alert to what those consequences might be. Although the example in the following paragraphs is from litigation, it illustrates the point well because the subject is familiar (torts and discrimination law), but the tax treatment is surprising.

Suppose you represent a plaintiff who has sued on claims of wrongful discharge and battery. The defendant offers to settle by paying an amount of money that satisfies your client, but the defendant prefers to pay the money entirely as back pay. He would rather be thought of as someone who fires an employee illegally than as someone who swings a tire iron while screaming "You're fired."

"It's a good amount of money," your client tells you. "Does it matter whether we call it back pay or damages for battery?"

"Yes," you reply. "It does matter. The $100,000 they're offering is worth only $65,000 because you'll pay federal and state income tax on it. But $100,000 in damages for battery is $100,000 because it's not taxed." If you fail to tell your client that, you've committed malpractice. And when you do say it, your client will probably send you back to tell the defendant that the money will be acceptable only as damages for battery.

You don't need to know the tax code from end to end. Instead, you need to know how tax law affects the types of transactions you deal with frequently. For example, a personal injury lawyer would know how tort recoveries are taxed. If you aren't experienced in the type of transaction you're doing, you need to be able to recognize *potential* tax issues and know when to get answers from a lawyer who specializes in tax.

## §2.6 OVERLAWYERING CAN BE AS HARMFUL AS UNDERLAWYERING

Underlawyering is doing a cursory or half-hearted job. Overlawyering is making an issue out of everything, whether it really matters or not.

Business people use the term *deal killers* to refer to lawyers who regularly overlawyer. Suppose that Dynamo Electric, Inc., a chain of retail stores, wants to rent a warehouse to store household appliances such as refrigerators and stereos. The most suitable warehouse is owned by Belinsky Properties, Inc. Dynamo talks to Belinsky, and they agree on how much rent Belinsky will receive and how many years Dynamo will occupy the building. Because a lease must be drawn up, each company calls in its lawyers. The lawyers start by arguing with each other over who will bear the risk of loss to Dynamo's merchandise if the warehouse burns down. This is a useful argument. Lawyers are paid to identify potential problems like that and then make sure harm is minimized.

But we're long past the point of diminishing returns when Belinsky's lawyer demands that Dynamo post a bond to indemnify Belinsky in case Belinsky is ever named as a defendant in a products liability suit concerning an appliance stored in the warehouse by Dynamo. When the clients learn this, Dynamo will think that if Belinsky is this unreasonable now, things will only get worse later. So Dynamo will instead rent a different warehouse from Franken & Partners. And Belinsky will want to know what went wrong.

"It isn't that the lawyers are actually trying to kill the deal. They just want to . . . dot the 'i's [and] cross the 't's . . . And they love to 'one-up' the other party's lawyers; in this game, being the last one to add a clause gains them great face."[2] This can get so bad that "some business people . . . never allow[] their own lawyer to talk to someone else's without supervision—the goal is to keep the lawyers from arguing back and forth until the contract is [too] long and the deal is dead."[3]

Focus on what's really needed to accomplish the client's goals. Provide just the right amount of lawyering to do that—not more and not less.

---

2. Nicholas Carroll, *Dancing with Lawyers: How to Take Charge and Get Results* 60 (1992).
3. *Id.* at 61.

## §2.7 PROFESSIONALISM IS A WAY OF BEING

*Transformation into a professional:* Becoming a professional is a long and gradual process, beginning in law school and continuing for years afterward. Throughout that time, you make choices about the kind of professional you'll be. Some of those choices are made in many small steps—so many and so small that you might not realize that they add up to important decisions. You've been making these choices since the first day of law school, when teachers began to pressure you to speak and listen—and to read and eventually write—with more precision than had ever been expected of you before. If you met that challenge, you've made some choices about the kind of lawyer you want to be, and you've probably become stronger for it and learned to see many things around you with greater clarity.

As you become a professional—an effective problem-solver, with excellent judgment and integrity, who communicates precisely, produces high-quality work reliably and efficiently, and accomplishes client goals with a minimum of supervision—you're becoming a different person. In their path-breaking lawyering skills textbook, Gary Bellow and Bea Moulton began with this quote from Robert Coles's biography of Erik Erikson:

> In this life we prepare for things, for moments and events and situations.... We worry about things, think about injustices, read what Tolstoi or Ruskin ... has to say.... Then, all of a sudden, the issue is not whether we agree with what we have heard and read and studied.... The issue is *us*, and what we have become.[4]

This is true for every lawyer, doctor, therapist, architect, or other professional. It's not just that a professional knows things that other people don't know or can use that knowledge. It's also that a professional thinks differently and sees the world differently. This issue is us—what kind of lawyer each of us has become or is becoming.

*Balance:* For many lawyers, it's a struggle to lead a balanced life—but it's a struggle you can win. Your family and the other people you care about are important. Each day that you don't spend time with them is a day you can't recover later. Lawyers who realize that in mid-career regret what they and their family and friends have missed. Do things that have nothing to do with law and that help you feel fulfilled as a human being. They refresh you and provide opportunities to be happier and more complete.

---

4. Gary Bellow & Bea Moulton, *The Lawyering Process: Materials for Clinical Instruction in Advocacy* 1 (1978), quoting from Robert Coles, *Erik H. Erikson, The Growth of His Work* 39 (1970).

# CHAPTER 3

# PROBLEM-SOLVING AND PROBLEM-PREVENTION

Lawyers solve existing problems and prevent future problems. That's what clients need. And truly top-notch lawyers—the most effective and capable ones you can find—don't narrowly "practice law." They're problem-solvers and problem-preventers in general. Law is just one of their tools.

## §3.1 DIAGNOSIS, PREDICTION, AND STRATEGY IN PROFESSIONAL WORK

Professionals *diagnose* what's happening now or has happened in the past. They *predict* what will happen in the future. And they create and implement *strategies* to influence events. This is true in all professions.

A lawyer diagnoses by figuring out why events are happening or have happened. Why is the client more upset over a small problem than a big one? Why is Norcomm, Inc. not making deliveries on time? In a negotiation, why is the other party unable to see that your proposal is good for both sides?

A lawyer predicts by prophesying how other people will react to events. How will the other party respond to a negotiation offer you contemplate making? If the client sues, how will a judge and jury react to the lawsuit (which is a more precise way of asking who will win)?

A *strategy* is a plan for resolving a problem favorably to the client—or, ideally, preventing the problem from even occurring. In litigation, this means a plan for winning. But in transactional work, it means a plan for reaching an agreement with the other party on terms that protect the client's interests. To strategize is to develop the plan. When you counsel a client, you offer plans as options from which the client can choose. When you prepare to negotiate, you develop a strategy for getting the other party to agree, as much as possible, to what your client needs.

Suppose the client is a developer who has signed a contract to buy a farm on which he had intended to build tract homes. Before the transaction could be completed, two things have happened. First, the local government has declared a five-year building moratorium because explosive development has outstripped the government's capacity to provide tap water and to process sewage. Second, the client has begun to suffer health problems. His family has persuaded him to go into semi-retirement. And he's entertaining the thought of living in the farmhouse and hiring neighboring farmers to farm the land rather than developing it for housing. The problem is that the contract includes the fields but not the farmhouse. The client has offered to buy the farmhouse as well, but the owners have refused. They don't care much about living in the farmhouse themselves. They believe its value will go up substantially in the future, and they simply want to sell it later rather than now. So the client would like to get out of this contract and buy some other farm.

In a client interview and afterward, you'll diagnose by learning the facts and figuring out how they affect the client legally, financially, and emotionally. To make the diagnosis concrete, you'll predict how people and courts will treat the client in the future. Based on the law, a prediction here might be this: *The contract is enforceable. If we sue for a court order rescinding it, we'll probably lose. If the client refuses to complete the purchase as required in the contract, and if the sellers sue for breach, they'll probably win, and the client will have to pay whatever damages they can prove.*

Don't give up yet. Lawyers are problem-solvers, and law is just one of their tools. Instead, develop strategic options that might protect the client despite his weak position in contract law. With the client, choose the best option based on your predictions of each strategy's likelihood of success and on the client's preferred style of addressing the problem. An effective strategy could involve converting conflict into an inclusive solution (§3.5) that satisfies everyone's needs. The developer's lawyer might say to her client:

> We could fight them in a lawsuit. But we'll probably lose, and your litigation expenses, including attorney's fees, would be at least $15,000 and could go as high as $120,000, and you'd have to pay them damages when you lose.
>
> But they don't seem to realize that this transaction is badly structured for them. If you and they go ahead with the deal as it's now structured, they'll pay a lot more tax than they need to. We can offer to renegotiate the whole deal to eliminate their unnecessary tax exposure, on condition that they agree to sell you the farmhouse at a reasonable price. If that works, it would solve this problem quickly and with as little conflict as possible.

As you implement your strategy, unexpected things can happen. If they're harmful, diagnose what's going wrong and restrategize by modifying the strategy or adopting a new one.

> When I called their lawyer and offered to renegotiate, the sellers blew a gasket and made a lot of threats about suing us. I've been trying to figure out why they'd react this way. They seemed to be thinking that we're trying to take advantage of them,

which makes no sense if they really understood the tax consequences. The sellers refused even to meet with us and sent word back through their lawyer that our choice is to go through with the deal as-is or get sued for damages.

I asked around, and the sellers don't have a reputation for being suspicious by nature. So I wondered just how much they really know about taxes in this kind of deal. I sent a letter to their attorney offering to pay for a consultation with any tax advisor they choose. We would not be present, and the only condition would be that the tax advisor be given a copy of the contract before meeting with the sellers. Because this was an offer in negotiation, their lawyer was ethically obligated to inform them of it.

It turns out that they had been doing their own taxes for years and had no idea what a mess they were about to get into. When a neutral tax advisor explained it to them, they realized that it made good financial sense to sell you the farmhouse now through a restructured deal that puts them in a better tax situation.

The lawyer's diagnosis of what was going wrong helped her restrategize and solve the problem.

Problem-prevention is problem-solving in advance. Effective lawyers develop the skill of foreseeing risk—predicting now that a problem will arise in the future if something isn't done now to prevent it, or at least reduce its harm if it does occur. Some risks are remote. They're so unlikely to happen that effort and client money would be wasted dealing with them now. Accurately assessing the odds of a problem occurring in the future is predictive thinking. *For most transactional lawyers, much of any day's work is problem-prevention.* For example, in lawyer-to-lawyer negotiated contracts—where lawyers negotiate the legal terms of the contract—each lawyer expends a lot of effort trying to reduce her client's future risk and thus prevent future problems.

For conciseness, this book uses the term *problem-solving* to cover both solving existing problems and preventing future ones.

## §3.2 HOW PROFESSIONALS DIAGNOSE, PREDICT, AND STRATEGIZE

The six steps of diagnosis, prediction, and strategy track the process of creativity, as established by empirical research.[1]

1. *Recognizing a problem and defining it.* Something is starting to go at least vaguely wrong. It takes an eye for trouble to notice this early and to bring it into focus, getting a clear idea of what it is. Consider what happened when the farmland sellers refused to renegotiate the contract. The developer's lawyer could have given up at that point, accomplishing nothing for her client. But she didn't give up. She considered their refusal to be a solvable problem rather than an unchangeable fact. A lawyer who's good at problem recognition is a lawyer who looks for problems rather than avoiding them.

---

1. See Teresa H. Amabile, *Creativity in Context: Update to the Social Psychology of Creativity* 119 (1996); John S. Dacey & Kathleen H. Lennon, *Understanding Creativity: The Interplay of Biological, Psychological, and Social Factors* 82–83, 173 (1998).

2. *Preparing: gathering and evaluating information and raw materials.* This includes discovering relevant law and facts in a fairly open-ended manner aided by an aggressive curiosity.
3. *Generating a range of options: hypotheses or potential solutions.* If you're diagnosing, imagine several potential explanations for the events in question (hypotheses). If you're predicting, imagine several potential prophesies of the future (also hypotheses). If you're strategizing, imagine several potential plans for influencing events (solutions). *The more possibilities you can generate here, the larger is the field you can choose from later.* In this stage, you're not verifying or judging each hypothesis or solution. That's the next step. Here, you're only listing possibilities.
4. *Evaluating options (hypotheses or potential solutions).* If you're diagnosing, test each possible explanation to see whether it accurately tells you why things are happening. If you're predicting, test each potential prophesy to estimate how likely it is to happen. If you're strategizing, test each plan for effectiveness: how well would it achieve the client's goals, at what cost, and with what risks? In all three activities, look for concrete, clarifying facts, evidence, and law. What would confirm that an explanation is accurate (if diagnosing), that a prophesy is likely to happen (if predicting), or that a plan will influence events (if developing a strategy)? Also, look for negative proof to reduce the number of hypotheses. What information could rule out an explanation or prophesy?
5. *Deciding.* Choose the most accurate diagnosis, the most likely prediction, or the most effective strategy.
6. *Acting.* If the decision is a diagnosis or a prediction, report it to whoever needs to know (the client, for example) or use it yourself for whatever purpose you had. If the decision is selection of a strategy, implement it.

In practice, the six stages aren't segmented as neatly as they appear here.

The thinking process can be recursive. There's a lot of circling back. As you evaluate hypotheses, for example, you might realize that you need to know some things you don't already know. So you go back into preparation to learn about those things and then return to evaluation. On the way, you might generate some other potential solutions. Or when you act on a solution, it might fail, and then you return to evaluating, or even to generating another solution.

Preparing and generating often happen at the same time. That can also be true of evaluating and deciding. And "the mind may be unconsciously incubating on one aspect" of a problem while "consciously . . . preparing for or verifying another aspect."[2] Ideas often surface into consciousness "unexpectedly, with surprising suddenness."[3] Professional work is an uneven mixture of "sudden bursts of insight and tiring efforts at execution."[4]

Don't be satisfied with the first reasonable hypothesis or solution you come up with. "In high-pressure situations, . . . most people seem to latch onto the first

---

2. Graham Wallas, *The Art of Thought* 81–82 (1926).
3. Teresa H. Amabile, *The Social Psychology of Creativity* 85 (1983).
4. Vera John-Steiner, *Notebooks of the Mind: Explorations of Thinking* 79 (1985).

plausible idea they get and push it as far as they can."[5] Clients need more than that. Work through the process of professional problem-solving.

Generating and evaluating pose the greatest challenges for students—in part because they require contrary skills. To generate the largest number of possible solutions or hypotheses, look under the surface of facts and law for deeper possibilities and meaning. Deactivate your skepticism. (You'll activate it again during the evaluation stage.) For now, think without inhibition.

All ideas have flaws. And many of those flaws can be fixed—later, after you've generated options. Ideas that might turn out to be good arrive together with ideas that might turn out to be wrong or even silly. If you criticize them as they arrive, they'll stop coming—all of them, the good as well as the bad—before you can understand their potential. *(Ideas fear rejection. If you were an idea, would you appear in the mind of a person eager to reject you?)* It's too easy to dismiss as foolish an incomplete hypothesis or solution that could become a better one if you let it stay long enough for you to work out its faults.

The skepticism on which evaluation depends is prized throughout the practice of law. It's taught in law school, and lawyers tend to be verbally aggressive. But a lawyer who is "more adept at criticizing ideas than at creating them"[6] will be, for that reason alone, a less effective problem solver. If you or someone else makes snap criticisms of your ideas as soon as they come up, your generating will be paralyzed. In any profession, hyper-criticism is dangerous because it shuts down the flow of ideas. When you see a lawyer, a student, or a teacher doing it, consider the damage it can cause. While generating ideas, don't be afraid of embarrassing yourself. Lon Fuller, the contracts scholar, wrote that generating stops when you ask yourself "anxiously at every turn that most inhibitive of questions, *'What will other people think?'*"[7]

Evaluating options, on the other hand, requires the qualities that would cripple generating: rigorous skepticism, a pragmatic sense of the realistic, a precise ability to calculate risk, and a fear that an idea might truly be foolish. Turn these qualities off while generating hypotheses and solutions. Then turn them back on once you've assembled a full range and are ready to start evaluating them. During generating, you'll do best if you think with intellectual freedom and a tolerance for chaos. But during evaluation, become a completely different kind of person, viewing things with the cold realism of one who must take responsibility for success or failure.

Evaluating options also depends on something that's not taught in most large law school classes: an accurate feel for how clients, judges, and juries make decisions and for how clients, judges, juries, witnesses, and opposing parties and their lawyers will react to things you do. Evaluating accurately requires a good intuition about people and situations to balance the analytical reasoning that law school has helped you develop. Analytical reasoning is useful up to a point. But it's not more valuable than emotional intelligence, especially the understanding of

---

5. John S. Dacey & Kathleen H. Lennon, *Understanding Creativity: The Interplay of Biological, Psychological, and Social Factors* (1998).
6. Paul Brest & Linda Krieger, *On Teaching Professional Judgment*, 69 Wash. L. Rev. 527, 541 (1994).
7. Lon Fuller, *On Teaching Law*, 3 Stan. L. Rev. 35, 43 (1950) (emphasis in original).

human nature that comes from empathy.[8] Good problem-solving involves all of you, not just the rational part.

Unless the circumstances are urgent, don't rush to make decisions. Premature judgment will cut off the earlier stages before they've done their work. The first good idea you come up with isn't typically the best idea you can find.

This book sometimes uses interchangeably the terms *potential solutions*, *choices*, and *options*. But not all choices or options are potential solutions. Where the client has suffered a loss, doing nothing is one of the options, and sometimes it's the only realistic one. But it doesn't solve the client's problem.

## §3.3 THINKING DIVERGENTLY AS WELL AS CONVERGENTLY

Convergent thinking progressively narrows an inquiry to find (converge onto) the single right answer. Divergent thinking is the opposite: broadening the inquiry by thinking in several directions to find many answers (or hypotheses or solutions). Here's the difference:[9]

*Convergent exam question:* Which of the following is commonly used in the manufacture of bricks?
(a) Cooled lava
(b) Clay
(c) Fossil oil
(d) Synthetic oil
*Correct answer:* (b).

*Divergent exam question:* In three minutes, think of as many uses for a brick or bricks as you can.
*Some possible answers:* to build steps, a walkway, or a garden border; to use as siding on a house exterior; to use as a paperweight on a desk; to hold down newspapers left at the curb for recycling; to throw at windows and break them; to circle a campfire so it doesn't spread while you sleep in a tent; to hold down the corners of the tent in a wind; to hide a secret message on a piece of paper folded underneath the brick; to throw at an opponent in a duel instead of shooting with a pistol; to block car wheels to keep the car from rolling away; to put in the trunk of a rear-wheel-drive car so it gets better traction in snow; to help weigh down a dead body thrown into a lake or stream; etc.

---

8. See Howard Gardner, *Multiple Intelligences* (2006); Daniel Goleman, *Emotional Intelligence* (2006).
9. See Malcolm Gladwell, *Outliers* 86–89 (2008).

The more uses, the more uninhibited your divergent thinking. If you came up with only a few uses, don't be discouraged. It's not your fault. For most students, education to this point has taught convergent thinking almost exclusively, largely omitting divergent thinking. Many students, when given an exercise like this, ask something like "We're allowed to think like that? Isn't the right answer the most important thing?" Yes, you're allowed to—and should—think like that. In professional practice, usually there's no one right answer. There are only good solutions.

You already know how to think convergently. It got you through college and into law school. Convergent thinking is measured in every standardized test, including the SAT, ACT, and LSAT. Every multiple-choice question in a course exam can be answered only through convergent thinking, and that's also true of most issues in law school essay exams. To gain basic and essential knowledge, you've had to learn correct answers (for example, negligence is the sum of duty, breach, injury, and proximate cause) and to separate what's correct from what isn't (breach of contract is not a tort). But if education were to stop there, it would be unrealistic and incomplete. Becoming a professional includes beginning to think divergently.

Generating options is divergent thinking. You start in one place (the problem), and you diverge—go out—in a number of directions. When lawyers solve real problems in the real world, they think divergently to come up with options. Then they think convergently to eliminate options that aren't practical or supported by the law or the facts. Option-evaluation is convergent thinking.

For many professionals, the opportunity to think divergently can introduce into professional work elements of play and fun. All the research into creativity—*all* the research—shows that people are more creative when they stop trying to separate play from work. Work is not inherently dreary.[10]

## §3.4 DEVELOPING A PROBLEM-SOLVING STYLE

It will take years to develop a problem-solving style that makes the best use of your strengths and limits the effect of your weaknesses. But here are some suggestions.

***Learn from experience.*** When you look back on a professional situation that turned out in a disappointing way, critique your own work. Did you fail to recognize points at which you could have made an important decision that might have altered the result? Was your preparation so cursory that you didn't have all the information you needed? Or was it so unnecessarily exhaustive that you didn't have time to do other things? Was there an hypothesis or solution that you became aware of too late because your generation was weak? Did you evaluate hypotheses or solutions accurately? When you decided, did you forget or ignore

---

10. See Mihaly Csikszentmihalyi, *Beyond Boredom and Anxiety: Experiencing Flow in Work and Play* (2000); Mihaly Csikszentmihalyi, *Flow: The Psychology of Optimal Experience* (2008); *Optimal Experience: Psychological Studies of Flow in Consciousness* (Mihaly Csikszentmihalyi & Isabella Selega Csikszentmihalyi, eds. 1988).

some of your evaluation? Or did other factors sneak in and influence the result? Looking at the big picture, how could you have done better?

If you're willing to be self-reflective, and if you scrutinize your own planning work with some regularity, you might notice some patterns. You can figure out which parts of the process come naturally to you and which parts you need to improve. Do you sometimes fail to notice opportunities to transform a situation? If so, you might try to improve your problem-recognition skills by disciplining yourself to look for those opportunities. Does important information seem to enter the picture too late to help you? During preparation, you might become more aggressive about figuring out exactly what you don't yet know and then filling those gaps. Does your idea-generation seem unproductive? Your well-developed critical and convergent thinking skills might be shutting down your imagination. Do you generate a large list of hypotheses and solutions but then tend to choose one with a fatal flaw in it? Perhaps those same critical thinking skills aren't helping you at the time when you really do need them: while evaluating and deciding.

Discover your strengths as well. What have you done effectively? If you understand your strengths, you know what you can capitalize on.

*Treat the entire problem as an integrated whole.* Step back far enough to see the big picture—the whole forest instead of only the individual trees—and keep that big picture in mind as you think about each smaller portion of the problem.

Sometimes all of a problem's aspects fit together into a single problem solvable through a strategy that addresses everything—if only the lawyer can see the entire problem as an integrated whole. Try to cultivate "peripheral vision": the "ability to see what is going on in the total environment, to understand how things connect. Lawyers with well-developed peripheral vision can be awesome in their ability to look at problems from many different perspectives, to see not only what is presented, but what is not presented."[11]

*Identify the few things that really matter.* An effective problem-solver identifies the very few things—facts, sentences in a contract, or legal rules—that are most likely to affect the way a client's situation is resolved. Of hundreds of relevant facts or points of law, in most instances, only very few—perhaps two or three or four—will affect results in the end. In the farmland example at the beginning of this chapter, none of the many relevant rules of contract law really mattered. Only one thing mattered: the sellers didn't realize how much tax they'd pay.

*Identify the decisive event (or events).* Effective strategies almost never consist of throwing everything at the other side and then awaiting further developments. The best strategies are based on accurate predictions that a particular kind of future event (or a small number of events) will cause a desired result—if only that event could be made to happen. You might think of it as the *decisive event* because its occurrence would effectively solve the problem.

Once the event is selected, strategic planning concentrates on causing it to occur. Organize your work to cause the decisive event or events by planning

---

11. Sallyanne Payton, *Is Thinking Like a Lawyer Enough?* 18 U. Mich. J.L. Reform 233, 241 (1985).

backward—from the future to the present—identifying the things that must be done to make the decisive event happen. Neustadt and May called this "backward mapping."[12]

For example, in the farmhouse problem earlier in this chapter, the decisive event was persuading the sellers that it would be to their own advantage to sell the farmhouse now rather than later. The law would neither force them to sell nor allow the client to escape the existing contract to buy the surrounding farmland, which the client now did not want without the farmhouse. From that insight, the lawyer mapped backward.

What would persuade the sellers that they would be better off selling the farmhouse now? Their reason for wanting to wait was financial: They assumed that the farmhouse would be worth more later. Their assumption created the client's problem. What might prove that assumption to be wrong or show it to be irrelevant? This line of questions led to the tax considerations. Treat the decisive event as a goal and then think from that goal back to the present so you can figure out what to *start* doing.

Don't just throw effort at the problem. Concentrate your work on whatever will be most likely to resolve the situation on desirable terms. Effort is wasted if diffused on other things. This is efficiency.

Develop one or more back-up strategies, in case the original strategy proves ineffective as a whole. You can identify alternative decisive events and strategize to cause them, in case they should become needed. Have a Plan B.

Because life is random, even chaotic, you'll never fully be in control of a situation. Problem-solving depends in part on the ability to integrate the unexpected into an *evolving* plan—to capitalize on accidents rather than be victimized by them. Sometimes a lawyer doesn't so much cause events as shepherd facts and circumstances so that they travel in the direction of the decisive event. Sometimes the lawyer doesn't even try to cause the decisive event. The event might be occurring anyway, independently of the lawyer's efforts—but without decisive effect unless the lawyer adds to it or alters it in some way. The lawyer's contribution would be to recognize the event's potential and do things that endow it with its decisive quality.

***Don't be afraid to take calculated risks.*** Recognize risks and decide when to take them and when to avoid them. Many problems can't be solved without risk taking. A *calculated* risk is one you take after weighing possible benefits and the odds of achieving them against potential harms and the odds of suffering them.

***Help your mind wander.*** Many professionals find that they have some of their best ideas when traveling to or from the office, when showering, when doing the dishes, or when jogging. What these have in common is that the professional is doing something mechanical, freeing the mind to wander.

***Resist the temptation to act on nonstrategic motivations.*** Act only after understanding how, in the situation at hand, your actions really will influence

---

12. Richard E. Neustadt & Ernest R. May, *Thinking in Time: The Uses of History for Decision-Makers* 255 (1986).

events. An action isn't strategic if its hidden function is to satisfy the lawyer's own emotional needs—for example, to hide fear, to create a reassuring illusion of doing something, to avoid admitting the error of earlier actions, to vent anger, or simply to reflect the lawyer's personality. What feels good isn't the same as what's strategically wise.

Most lawyers have some personal trait that, if left uncontrolled, will obstruct problem-solving in one way or another. An example is the confrontational personality that confuses hostility, voice raising, and table pounding with problem-solving. Sometimes a staged display of anger is strategically appropriate to communicate that the other side's actions are unacceptable. But just as often, it can be counter-productive. Lawyers who automatically seek self-fulfillment through confrontation are usually not thinking through the process of problem-solving. The express-train roar of a confrontational lawyer at full throttle is often the equivalent of "strategic bluster"[13] camouflages the confrontational lawyer's own anxiety and perplexity.

When you're attacked by a confrontational lawyer, you may have advantages. It might not feel that way, especially if you're a young professional verbally ambushed by an intimidating and more experienced practitioner. Consider what's really going on. Loud, bellicose talk often means either that the talker knows he's in a weak position or that he's too confrontational to be a good strategist. (The older lawyer may have other advantages, however, such as a more thorough knowledge of your client's industry.)

## §3.5 THE INCLUSIVE SOLUTION

In an influential book titled *In a Different Voice*, Carol Gilligan differentiates between the ethic of justice and the ethic of care, illustrated through the responses of two children to a hypothetical that poses a moral problem.[14] Jake and Amy are 11 years old and, in interviews, have been asked to state their opinions on Heinz's dilemma: Heinz's wife is ill, and her life can be saved only with a drug that costs more money than Heinz and his wife have. The local druggist refuses to lower his price. Jake and Amy have been asked whether Heinz should steal the drug. Jake answers yes, because

> a human life is worth more than money . . . . [*Why is life worth more than money?*] Because the druggist can get a thousand dollars later from rich people with cancer, but Heinz can't get his wife again. . . . [If Heinz is caught], the judge would probably think it was the right thing to do.[15]

Jake says that Heinz's dilemma is "a math problem with humans."[16]

Jake reasons exactly the way students are taught to think in law school, through a hierarchy of principles. Some principles are more important than—and therefore trump—other principles. Jake "spots the legal issues of excuse and

---

13. Michael Sherry, *The Slide to Total Air War*, The New Republic, Dec. 16, 1981, at 20, 23.
14. Carol Gilligan, *In a Different Voice* 25–37 (1982).
15. *Id.* at 26.
16. *Id.*

justification, balances the rights, and reaches a decision, while considering implicitly, if not explicitly, the precedential effect of his decision."[17] This sounds as close as an eleven-year-old can get to legal analysis. But it's not the best way to solve a real-life problem.

> Amy says that Heinz should not steal the drug:
> I think there might be other ways besides stealing it, like if he could borrow the money . . . , but he really shouldn't steal the drug—but his wife shouldn't die, either. [*Why shouldn't he steal the drug?*] If he stole the drug, he might save his wife then, but if he did, he might have to go to jail, and then his wife might get sicker again, and he couldn't get more of the drug. . . . So they should really just talk it out and find some other way to make the money.[18]

In the rest of her response, Amy focuses on the relationships between Heinz and his wife and between them and the druggist. In Gilligan's words:

> Amy envisions the wife's continuing need for her husband and the husband's continuing concern for his wife and seeks to respond to the druggist's need in a way that would sustain rather than sever connection. . . . Since Amy's moral judgment is grounded in the belief that, "if somebody has something that would keep somebody alive, then it's not right not to give it to them," she considers the problem in the dilemma to arise not from the druggist's assertion of rights but from his failure of response.[19]

Jake "speaks about equality, reciprocity, fairness, rights," while Amy "speaks about connection, not hurting, care, and response."[20] Amy "fights the hypo" and "wants to know more facts: Have Heinz and the druggist explored other possibilities, like a loan or credit transaction? Why couldn't Heinz and the druggist simply sit down and talk it out so that the druggist would come to see the importance of Heinz's wife's life?"[21]

Don't dismiss Amy's thinking as naive. Jake might do better in a law school classroom. But Amy might be a better lawyer because she's the more effective problem-solver. Jake has responded to what he believes to be a question about hierarchical logic, which would determine who wins and who loses. Amy wants to find a way for nobody to lose. She's searching for a *solution*, rather than a way of scoring who's more right.

Amy is close to finding the decisive event. She wants to help the druggist understand, in his heart, the wife's desperate situation or, if that doesn't work, to persuade other people to help. What Jake heard as a question about hierarchical score-keeping, Amy heard as a question about solving a problem. When she "fights the hypo," it's because she's perceptive enough to recognize that the problem doesn't necessarily require a decision about whose rights are more important. She resists the constrictions imposed by the interviewer, and her

---

17. Carrie Menkel-Meadow, *Portia in a Different Voice: Speculations on a Women's Lawyering Process*, 1 Berkeley Women's L.J. 39, 46 (1985).
18. Gilligan, *supra* note 14, at 28.
19. *Id.* at 28.
20. Remarks by Gilligan in *Feminist Discourse, Moral Values, and the Law—A Conversation*, 34 Buff. L. Rev. 11, 44 (1985).
21. Menkel-Meadow, *supra* note 17, at 46.

solution-generation process is richer because she tries to break out of the interviewer's preconceptions.

Here's an example in which one lawyer reasons like Jake and fails, while another lawyer reasons like Amy and succeeds:

> [A] lawyer who came to my office . . . presented this problem to me as an attorney for a local bank. Where the signature card required A, B, and C to sign, and C refused because of a disagreement with B, what kind of court order would permit the bank to release the funds? Since any court proceeding is relatively involved and expensive (and also since I had not the faintest idea what kind of an order could be obtained), I suggested that we broaden the problem definition to, "In what ways might we obtain the release of the funds?" [That led to] an effective method of convincing C to sign the withdrawal slip. *What turned out to be the best solution had simply not occurred to the [first] attorney because he had limited himself to the narrow "court order" definition of the problem.*[22]

Amy's solution-evaluation is more realistic than Jake's because she looks for what Gilligan calls "the inclusive solution"[23]—the one that solves the problem by satisfying the needs of everyone involved. Her focus on relationships helps her realize that Heinz isn't really free of his dilemma until the druggist is as well.

Perhaps with some oversimplification, the end of Amy and Jake's reasoning—as seen on the evening news—would be Amy's announcement of the kind of fundraising that touches everyone's heart and wallet, while Jake desperately tries to persuade a judge and jury not to send his client to prison.

In the farmhouse problem at the beginning of this chapter, the lawyer's solution was inclusive: It solved her client's problem and eliminated conflict by solving at the same time a problem that the other parties didn't realize they had. The most satisfying solutions are the ones that leave no losers.

---

22. Gordon MacLeod, *Creative Problem-Solving—For Lawyers?!* 16 J. Legal Educ. 198, 201 (1963) (italics added).
23. Remarks by Gilligan, *supra* note 20, at 45.

# CHAPTER 4

# ORAL COMMUNICATION SKILLS

*How you say something has an enormous effect on the way people respond.* Words that seem to convey approximately the same idea may actually have separate meanings with a precise difference between them ("curious" and "nosy," for example). Or they might mean the same thing, but with different connotations (such as "dirty" and "filthy").

Senior lawyers greatly value the ability to communicate orally. When law firm hiring partners were surveyed about the skills they expected new law school graduates to have mastered before they start work, 91 percent of them mentioned oral communication.[1]

## §4.1 LISTENING AND—MORE IMPORTANT—HEARING

*The ability to listen well is as important in the practice of law as the ability to talk well.* The common image of a lawyer is of a person talking—to juries, to judges, to adversaries, to reporters. But the lawyer who knows how to listen has a tremendous advantage. The most effective way to learn what people know and think is to listen carefully to what they say.

"Listening," says playwright and actor Anna Deavere Smith, "is not just hearing what someone tells you word for word. You have to listen with a heart. . . . It is very hard work."[2] "Listening," adds Nance Guilmartin, "isn't just about being

---

1. Bryant Garth & Joanne Martin, *Law Schools and the Construction of Competence*, 43 J. Legal Educ. 469, 490 (1993).
2. Karen W. Arenson, *The Fine Art of Listening: Anna Deavere Smith Helps NYU Law Students Look Beyond the Legal Questions*, N.Y. Times, Jan. 13, 2002, Educ. Life at 34, 35.

quiet. It's about listening to what people say, what they don't say, and what they mean. . . . Listening is about hearing with our eyes, our ears, and our heart. . . ."[3] Listening includes deciphering the person who's speaking. What matters to her as a person? How does she see the world? If you don't ask yourself these questions, you won't understand the full meaning behind her words.

Some lawyers talk too much and listen too little. Below is an example. This client has been in the lawyer's office for less than five minutes and is now beginning to explain why he's there:

*Client:* I was walking down the street and found a big envelope.
*Lawyer:* What did it look like?
*Client:* Tan colored, eight-and-a-half by eleven inches. It was lying right there on the pavement. It looked full of something, so I picked it up.
*Lawyer:* Have you ever done this before?
*Client:* No.
*Lawyer:* What did you do after you picked it up?
*Client:* I looked inside and saw money. I looked around for somebody who might have dropped it.
*Lawyer:* You want to know whether you can keep the money?
*Client:* Oh, no.

Here's what the client would have said if the lawyer had listened instead of talking:

*Client:* I was walking down the street and found a big envelope. It was lying right there on the pavement. It looked full of something, so I picked it up. There was a lot of money in it but no name or address on it. I looked around for somebody who might have dropped it, but nobody seemed to be looking for something. I waited about 15 minutes, but nothing happened. I was late for a dentist appointment, so I left. At home that night, I counted the money. It was $10,000 exactly. I read the newspapers carefully for a week to see if anybody was reported to have lost the money, and nobody was. I'd like to donate it to a shelter for homeless people. Can I legally do that?

Listening is hard work and a skill that can be learned. It includes listening with your eyes: what is the other person telling you through attire, facial expression, or body position? You can listen more effectively if you ask yourself these questions while the other person is talking:

What words—exactly—am I hearing, and what do those words mean?
What do the speaker's words imply (hint at)?
What do the speaker's tone of voice and body language (facial expression, posture, etc.) imply?
*Why* is the speaker saying or implying these things?
What is the speaker *not* saying or implying that other people in her situation might often communicate? Why?

---

3. Nance Guilmartin, *Healing Conversations* xx (2002).

## §4.2 ACTIVE LISTENING

Passive listening is hearing what's being said and thinking about it. That's fine as long as the client does a good job of telling the story and believes that you care. Active listening, on the other hand, is a way of encouraging talk without asking questions. It also reassures a client that what she's saying has an effect on you. In active listening, you participate in the conversation by reflecting back what you hear.

Compare these three examples:

*1. A lawyer listens passively.*

    *Client:* I wanted to buy a very reliable car with a manual transmission and a sunroof. The car has to be reliable. I can't spare the time to take it into the shop any more than necessary. You can't get a sunroof and a manual transmission from Toyota. You can at Honda, but the dealer didn't have any cars in stock. I had to special order it. I gave them a $5,000 deposit. Two months later, they called to tell me the car had arrived. But it had an automatic transmission and no sunroof. I told them that wasn't the car I ordered. They refused to return the deposit and said I had to accept the car. I don't want it. A sunroof helps cool off the car quickly, and in the winter it lets in light and makes the car feel roomier. And a manual transmission makes the car more fun to drive.

*2. Another lawyer listens actively:*

    *Client:* I wanted to buy a very reliable car with a manual transmission and a sunroof. The car has to be reliable. I can't spare the time to take it into the shop any more than necessary. You can't get a sunroof and a manual transmission from Toyota. You can at Honda, but the dealer didn't have any cars in stock. I had to special order it. I gave them a $5,000 deposit. Two months later, they called to tell me the car had arrived. But it had an automatic transmission and no sunroof.
    *Lawyer:* Really.
    *Client:* I was astounded. I told them that wasn't the car I ordered. They refused to return the deposit and said I had to accept the car!
    *Lawyer:* You must have been pretty upset.
    *Client:* Absolutely. I don't want the car. A sunroof helps cool off the car quickly, and in the winter it lets in light and makes the car feel roomier.
    *Lawyer:* They are nice.
    *Client:* And a manual transmission makes the car more fun to drive.

*3. A third lawyer listens with a tin ear:*

    *Client:* I wanted to buy a very reliable car with a manual transmission and a sunroof. The car has to be reliable. I can't spare the time to take it into the shop any more than necessary. You can't get a sunroof and a manual transmission from Toyota. You can at Honda, but the dealer didn't have any cars in stock. I had to special order it. I gave them a $5,000 deposit. Two months later, they called to tell me the car had arrived. But it had an automatic transmission and no sunroof. I told them that wasn't the car I ordered.

*Lawyer:* Did you sign a contract that specified that the car had to have a sunroof and a manual transmission?

*Client:* I didn't sign anything except the $5,000 check. They refused to return the deposit and said I had to accept the car.

*Lawyer:* Is the car defective in some way, or is it just not the car you want?

*Client:* I don't want it. It's not what I ordered, and I shouldn't have to accept it. I want a sunroof and a manual transmission. A sunroof helps cool off the car quickly, and in the winter it lets in light and makes the car feel roomier. A manual transmission makes the car more fun to drive.

In the first example, the client tells the story without any reaction from the lawyer. This is fine for a while. But eventually, and maybe soon, most clients would become distressed without any response from the lawyer.

In the second example, the lawyer's interjections show understanding and empathy and encourage the client to continue. But notice that the lawyer waits before saying anything. That's because, if the lawyer has the patience to listen, the client will often volunteer information the lawyer might not otherwise ask about. The first time the lawyer interjects is the first time that simple courtesy would demand an acknowledgment of the client's predicament. Before that point, it's often better to confine active listening to nonverbal support, such as nods and eye contact.

But in the third example, the lawyer interrupts destructively, derailing the client and putting her on the defensive. Although the lawyer asks questions, those questions obstruct information rather than eliciting it. If this continues much longer the client may shut down. When lawyers converse in this way, they elevate rational needs for explanations over human needs.

People provide information more readily to someone with whom they feel a sense of connection. And people more readily sense connection when they feel heard and understood.

## §4.3 ASKING QUESTIONS

*An effective lawyer asks the most productive questions in the most productive way.* A good question is artistic. It cuts through a mountain of debris to find hidden treasure. An effective lawyer asks good questions constantly.

Ask for all the important information. Good questions seek things of value, things that really do need to be known. Some people can fill an hour with marginal questions. Others can learn everything in five minutes.

Use the words that are most likely to produce valuable information. Some words help find information and encourage answers, while other words confuse, cloud memory, or provoke resistance.

Decide when to ask *narrow questions* and when to ask *broad questions*. A narrow question asks for specific information ("What time did your plane arrive?"). A broad question asks for general information and often invites the person answering the question to decide what to emphasize ("How was your trip?").

If you need to know something specific, a narrow question is the fastest way to find out. If you're not sure what's important, a broad question can produce a lot of information, which you can then begin to sort out. Often (but not always), it's more effective to start with broad questions and then work toward narrow ones.

Decide when to ask *leading questions* and when to ask *nonleading questions*. A leading question not only suggests the answer; it also creates pressure to provide that answer.

"You've just returned from Bermuda, haven't you?" is a leading question. Expect the questioner to be surprised—and perhaps unhappy—if you answer no.

"Have you been to Bermuda lately?" is a narrow, nonleading question. It's narrow because it asks for specific information (see above). It's nonleading because the wording implies that the questioner would be satisfied with either yes or no, as long as it's truthful.

"Would you tell me about any trips you might have taken recently?" is a broad nonleading question. It's broad because it asks about traveling in general and not just to Bermuda. It's nonleading because, again, the wording implies that the questioner would be happy with any truthful answer.

Leading questions are useful in two situations. The first is when you think you know the answer and are using the question just to raise a topic so you can then ask other questions to learn things you don't already know:

"You've just returned from Bermuda, haven't you?" [*a leading question*]
"Yes."
"What's it like to visit Bermuda at this time of year?" [*a broad nonleading question*]

The second situation is when you're trying to pin something down or extract a factual concession:

"You've just returned from Bermuda, haven't you?" [*a leading question*]
"Yes."
"And while you were in Bermuda, you explored the possibility of avoiding U.S. taxes by incorporating off-shore, didn't you?" [*another leading question*]

Be *patient*. Patience, as Henry Aaron said, is "the art of waiting."[4] Some lawyers have not mastered this art. If they don't get an instantaneous answer to a question, they ask another one immediately. The other person might have been thinking about the first question and on the verge of giving an interesting and useful answer. But the second question cut that off. Because of impatience, the lawyer might never learn the answer to the first question.

Let silence help you. Suppose you ask a question and hear nothing in response. Actually, you do hear something. You hear the silence of the other person

---

4. Henry Aaron with Lonnie Wheeler, *If I Had a Hammer: The Hank Aaron Story* 236 (paperback ed. 1992). (Aaron hit 755 home runs in part by waiting for the right pitch.)

deciding how to answer. Listen to the silence, and wait. If you dislike silence, the other person might, too. And the other person's dislike of silence might cause her to produce lots of information. Be patient.

Listen carefully to answers and ask complete lines of questions. Suppose you ask a question on Topic A and get some of the information you asked for. If you imitate the interviewers you see on television, you'll ignore the missing information and ask an unrelated question on Topic B. But if you act like a good lawyer, you won't go on to Topic B without asking all the follow-up questions necessary to get all the information you need on Topic A. Find out everything you'll need. Not just a lot of things. *Everything.*

## §4.4 COMMUNICATING EMPATHY

Empathy is feeling what another person feels. Sympathy is more common and less valuable than empathy. "If you are sympathetic to others, your heart goes out to them, and you feel compassion, but these are *your* feelings. You don't know what *they're* feeling.... If you are empathetic to others, you are not merely feeling sorry for them but are projecting yourself into their hearts, as though you are sensing what it's like to be in their shoes."[5]

A struggling rock musician recalled two conversations about his difficulties. The first was with a successful performer named Timmy, the brother of a friend:

> My band had played only fifteen shows in the previous year, and even those had been sparsely attended. Regardless of how much we practiced and promoted our shows, we couldn't generate a dedicated following.
>
> When I told this to Timmy, he simply shrugged his shoulders and said, "Let me tell you about my experience. If you rock, the crowds will double every week and someone will offer you a deal. No way I'd do fifteen gigs without having a big crowd. You're in a real bad place there."
>
> To this day I still remember how terrible I felt after that conversation.
>
> In contrast, a week later I met a musician named Joe, the bass player in a successful local reggae band. I shared my problems with Joe, too. Although he was also successful, Joe, trying hard to understand how I felt, blurted out *how uncomfortable he knew it must be to stand in front of those small crowds*.... Was there anything he could do to help?
>
> For years I basked in the glow of his kindness....[6]

Empathy is essential in interviewing, counseling, and negotiating. Empathy helps you discover who your clients are as people and what they're really feeling. Once they sense true empathy from you, they'll tell you more because you've earned their trust. And empathy from a lawyer can help a client feel stronger and more capable of dealing with the issues the client has brought to the lawyer.

Even in negotiation, empathy can be helpful, but in carefully chosen spots. Empathy at the right moment can break logjams and facilitate collaborative problem-solving. When the other lawyer or the other party feels understood by

---
5. Tim Sanders, *The Likeability Factor* 117 (2005).
6. *Id.* at 121 (italics added).

you, often they're willing to reciprocate and try to understand what you need for your client.

But empathy has to be authentic. If you pretend to be empathetic, people will sense that it's not genuine and will feel uncomfortable.

## ▪ §4.5 PAINTING A PICTURE

When you paint a picture, you use words to create a scene in the listener's mind. The listener will have to use a little imagination to see the scene, but the more details you provide and the more vivid your words, the easier it will be for the listener to see your scene.

In negotiation, you might paint this picture, which the other party, a manufacturer of electronics gadgets, might find intriguing:

> As you know, my client has developed a patent-protected device that silences automobile security alarms within a range of 400 feet.
>
> Although people install these things in their cars, studies show that car thieves are not deterred by them. Nearly every time you hear a car alarm, it has been set off accidentally by electrical malfunction, by a thunderclap, by another car tapping the alarmed car while parking, or even by somebody leaning against the alarmed car. Everybody knows that. So when a car alarm goes off, nobody thinks a car is being stolen. The only thing the alarm accomplishes is to annoy neighbors.
>
> If you and my client agree on a price, my client would license this device to you exclusively. You would be the only manufacturer in the world selling a product that could be used to stop this ear-shattering racket.
>
> Suppose you live near a parking lot or a street with a lot of parked cars. Every once in a while, one of these alarms goes off in the middle of the night. You were asleep but suddenly you sit bolt upright in bed. If the alarm doesn't turn itself off in a minute or two, you'll listen to it for a long time and won't be able to go back to sleep. Even if it does turn itself off quickly, you won't be rested the next day because rest happens only with uninterrupted sleep.
>
> This doesn't have to happen. Before you get into bed in the first place, you turn on my client's device. Then you go to sleep confident that you will sleep through the night. Our market surveys suggest that to get this benefit people are willing to pay . . .

From this, can you imagine a television commercial for the product?

## ▪ §4.6 USING TONE OF VOICE AND BODY LANGUAGE

Some things can't be communicated very clearly or naturally in words. Suppose that a client is a charming and witty person whose presence you enjoy. If you say exactly that to the client, both of you might feel uncomfortable. But if you smile and speak in a friendly tone whenever you see the client, the message gets across much more naturally. (It's appropriate to use words to compliment the client on qualities more directly related to your collaboration. If the client is realistic, reasonable, creative, or perceptive when you work together, it's appropriate to mention those things.)

Suppose that in negotiation the other lawyer has just made a proposal that seems to ignore everything you've said about your client's needs. You will make things worse if you say, "You blockhead! Didn't you understand anything I've told you about my client?" That would introduce pointless interpersonal conflict. And words alone aren't getting through to this lawyer anyway. You might say, "For the reasons I've explained before, that will not satisfy any of my client's needs," while using a tone of voice and perhaps a facial expression to suggest that the negotiation will fail unless the adversary becomes more responsive.

When are tone of voice and body language better than words? Sometimes, words will make one or both people uncomfortable (as with the charming and witty client). And sometimes, words that convey all you feel will make it hard for the other person to change behavior (as with the lawyer who hasn't been listening to you). Tone of voice and body language can be used to imply in situations where explicitly saying something would cause additional problems.

## §4.7 MAKING ARGUMENTS

An argument is a group of ideas expressed logically to convince a listener to do what you need. You already know a lot about how to do this.

A sign of *in*effectiveness in a lawyer is a tendency to make arguments in situations where it would be more productive to do the things explained in this chapter—listen, ask questions, empathize, paint a picture, or imply through tone of voice or body language. Nobody really knows why ineffective lawyers argue when they shouldn't. It might be because argument is one of the first communication tools taught in law school, which could leave students with the impression that arguing is the essence of lawyering.

Certainly, every lawyer needs to know how to make persuasive arguments. Sometimes the only way, or the most effective way, to get what the client needs is through argument. But a threshold skill is knowing *when* to argue and when to do something else instead.

# PART II

# WORKING WITH TRANSACTIONAL CLIENTS

# CHAPTER 5

# LAWYERING FOR AND WITH CLIENTS

## §5.1 CLIENT-CENTERED LAWYERING

A client is not an item of work. You probably dislike it when a doctor treats you as a case of flu rather than as a human being who has the flu. And the problem is more than unpleasantness: a doctor who treats you *as a human being with flu-like symptoms* might spend enough time with you to learn that you also have other symptoms, and that you therefore do not have the flu, but instead another disease, which should be treated differently.

The opposite of treating the client as an item of work is "client-centered lawyering," a phrase that originated in a ground-breaking book by David Binder and Susan Price.[1] It means focusing our efforts around what the client wants and treating the client as an effective collaborator. A client has to live with the results of our work long after the work and the client have faded into the back of our memory.

A client who isn't experienced at hiring lawyers is very different from the client who hires lawyers routinely. The inexperienced client may have more anxiety and will need to learn how to work with lawyers. The experienced client may have more sharply defined goals and may think of hiring a lawyer as bringing in a specialist to perform a narrowly defined task.

---

1. David A. Binder & Susan M. Price, *Legal Interviewing and Counseling: A Client-Centered Approach* (1977). A more recent version is David A. Binder, Paul Bergman, Paul R. Trembley & Ian S. Weinstein, *Lawyers as Counselors: A Client-Centered Approach* (3d ed. 2011).

## §5.2 THE CLIENT AS A COLLEAGUE AND COLLABORATOR

Consider two scenes in two different lawyers' offices. In one, the lawyer sits behind a large desk and the client sits in a chair on the opposite side of the desk. When the client speaks, it's to supply facts the lawyer has asked for. When the lawyer speaks, it is to provide professional advice. This is a traditional model of the attorney-client relationship: the passive client protected by the powerful professional.

In the second scene, the lawyer and client sit together, perhaps at a conference table. They brainstorm, go over documents, and talk about which of several possible strategies would best accomplish the client's goals—and in doing so, they're both active. This has been called the participatory model of the attorney-client relationship. The lawyer assumes that she doesn't have all the answers, and the client is enlisted to supply an added measure of creativity and an often superior knowledge of the facts.

Most clients want lawyers who know how to use the participatory model, although a significant minority of clients still prefer the traditional version. The reverse was probably true 40 or 50 years ago. Some clients who still prefer the traditional model do so because they feel reassured turning things over to a trusted authority figure.

In transactional work, many businesses prefer to turn things over to a lawyer and let the lawyer proceed as she thinks best. That might look like the traditional model, but it usually isn't. These clients aren't submitting to their lawyers. They're close to doing the opposite. They believe the lawyer is no better than an equal, and they might feel that the lawyer is a subordinate. The lawyer has been hired for her expertise, and the client is a busy person who has little time to spare for collaborative problem-solving. The client expects the lawyer to produce results while taking up client time only to the extent necessary.

Thus, in transactional work the participatory model has two versions: a collaborative version, portrayed in the second scene above, and a business-efficient version. The client's needs and desires will determine the version used. And those needs and desires can change during the representation. A client who normally wants the business-efficient version might find it necessary, during a crisis, to invest time and effort in collaboration, switching back to a business-efficient relationship afterward.

In a pioneering study, Douglas Rosenthal studied personal injury cases to determine whether one model produces better solutions than the other.[2] Rosenthal examined a number of cases, categorized the plaintiff's attorney-client relationship in each case as either traditional or participatory, and compared the result in each case with an independent evaluation of what the plaintiff's claim was worth. On average, the participatory plaintiff's lawyers got better results. The gap between the participatory and the traditional results was not huge, and Rosenthal's sample was relatively small. But since then, it has become widely believed that participatory relationships with clients produce better and more satisfying results than traditional relationships do.

---

2. Douglas E. Rosenthal, *Lawyer and Client: Who's in Charge?* (1974).

Why does the collaborative version of the participatory model seem to work better and to satisfy more clients and lawyers than the traditional model described in the first scene at the beginning of this section? A client's insights are valuable, and a lawyer and client working together will come up with more and better solutions than the lawyer working alone. In addition, lawyers are human and make mistakes. An actively involved client will catch at least some of those mistakes before they cause harm. Many clients can understand more of how to solve their problems than some lawyers give them credit for. And most clients know at least as much or even more about their own needs than a lawyer will. Participatory lawyering also respects clients' dignity and self-responsibility. It can help to reduce the anxiety a client might feel if kept in the dark about what the lawyer is doing. And it protects "the integrity of professionals by liberating them from . . . the burdens imposed [by a] paternal role" and from client suspicion fueled by the client's ignorance about what the lawyer is doing.[3]

But the collaborative version of the participatory model also carries some burdens. In business, the main burden is time. A business person whose day is already filled with pressing matters has learned to be time-efficient and expects lawyers to do the same. An example is this phone call:

*Lawyer:* On the Clayton matter, I'm about to do X. In response, Clayton will probably do Y. Is there any reason not to do X?
*Client:* Have you thought about Z?
*Lawyer:* Yes. If Z happens, we can handle it.
*Client:* Go ahead.

Total elapsed time—including hello and goodbye—would be a minute or two. This is participatory even though it might not look like it. The client wants to be consulted but only when the issue is worth the time it will consume. Notice how concisely these two people speak to each other. They can communicate so much in so few words because they know how to be efficient and each trusts the other's judgment.

The client sees Z as a risk and wants to make sure it's being dealt with. Told that it is, the client authorizes the lawyer to proceed. Here a busy executive is treating the lawyer as a trusted subordinate who knows how to use the executive's time efficiently. A different client—one who isn't an executive or has not yet come to trust the lawyer's judgment—would want much more participation in decisions.

In a traditional lawyer-client relationship, the lawyer would not have made this phone call at all and instead would have done X without consulting the client. If the client had known of a reason why X would have been a bad idea, the traditional lawyer might have caused a disaster. That's one of the reasons why participatory lawyer-client relationships tend to produce better results.

Where the client is a busy person, the participatory lawyer has to limit conversations like this to issues the client will consider crucial. In transactional work, *client* is a relative term. If an organization retained the lawyer, the organization is the client in a legal sense. But in a human sense, the client is the person or people

---

3. *Id.* at 169.

in the organization who make the decisions regarding the matter on which the lawyer is working. In the phone conversation quoted above, if the person the lawyer called is an executive vice president in a large corporation, the action the lawyer is about to take had better be earth-shaking. Otherwise, the lawyer has wasted the executive VP's time. But if the person the lawyer called is a lower-level manager who supervises 30 employees in the same corporation—or the owner of a small business with ten employees—X can be much less important and still justify the conversation.

More extended participatory discussions, in the range of an hour or more, are typical where any of the following are true: the client hasn't dealt with lawyers frequently in the past; the client has little experience with this type of transaction; the transaction is, from the client's point of view, very important; the legal issues are complicated and are interwoven with facts the client must supply and the decisions the client must make.

## §5.3 WHO DECIDES WHAT

The law of professional responsibility and malpractice provide that certain decisions are reserved to the client and may not be made by the lawyer. If the lawyer makes decisions reserved to the client, the lawyer can be disciplined under the rules of professional responsibility, held liable in malpractice, or both.

Legally, the client defines the goals of the representation, while the lawyer decides what the Model Rules of Professional Conduct calls "technical, legal, and tactical issues."[4] Nearly all examples in the case law and the Model Rules refer not to transactional work but instead to litigation decisions such as where to sue, what theory of the case to advocate, what evidence to submit and witnesses to call, and what arguments to make. The case law allows a lawyer to make those litigation decisions unilaterally, without consulting the client, or even over the client's objections. (But if you do such a thing, the case law will not stop the client from firing you and telling every other potential client why.)

Because so few transactional situations appear in the case law and Model Rules, you'll have to reason by analogy to the types of litigation decisions listed in the preceding paragraph. One transactional situation, however, is clear cut on its own terms: correcting a scrivener's error, which is an inaccurate expression in a written contract of what the parties have agreed to. A lawyer is ethically obligated to correct a scrivener's error even if the client objects (see §16.1 for why).

In other respects, however, the Model Rules of Professional Conduct require not only that a lawyer "abide by a client's decisions concerning the objectives of representation [but also] consult with the client as to the means by which they are to be pursued."[5] And the Model Rules suggest that the lawyer defer to the client when technical and tactical decisions raise "such questions as the expense to be incurred and concern for third persons who might be adversely affected."

Even for questions that by law a lawyer can decide unilaterally, you should consult with the client anyway if there's a possibility that the client might be able

---

4. Model Rules of Professional Conduct, Comment to Rule 1.2(a).
5. Rule 1.2(a).

to add information or ideas or if the client might have preferences about how the question is handled. If in doubt, err on the side of consulting with the client. Not only does consultation improve the odds of getting good results, but it reduces the chances of friction between lawyer and client. Lawyers who regularly communicate with clients seem to have fewer ethics complaints and malpractice actions brought against them.

## §5.4 WHAT CLIENTS LIKE AND DISLIKE IN A LAWYER

Charles Dickens's novel *Bleak House*[6] tells the story of a lawsuit to divide up an estate. The suit has "become so complicated that no man alive knows what it means."[7] All the parties to the suit are oppressed by it. One of them complains, "We are always appearing, and disappearing, and swearing, and interrogating, and filing, and cross-filing, and arguing, and sealing, and motioning, and referring, and reporting. . . . Law finds it can't do this, Equity finds it can't do that; neither can so much as say it can't do anything, without this solicitor instructing and this counsel appearing for A, and that solicitor instructing and that counsel appearing for B; and so on through the whole alphabet."[8]

Finally, nearly 800 pages later, the lawyers declare that the suit is over because the estate is now empty, everything in it having been spent on lawyers' fees.[9] This is the subliminal fear of everyone with a problem that might have something to do with the law—that hiring a lawyer leaves the client with two problems. The first will be the original problem, and the second will be the lawyer.

Clients worry constantly about the cost of legal work. An efficient lawyer who finds ways to reduce costs can earn the loyalty of clients. A lawyer who can't do that risks losing clients to the first kind of lawyer. Loyal clients recommend their lawyer to others. Those recommendations can be far more persuasive than advertising on billboards or television.

Clients dislike lawyers who make promises they cannot keep, brag, speak in legal jargon, are condescending, and talk too much and listen too little. Clients hate having to fight to get their lawyers' attention. A study showed that how doctors talk to patients is the strongest predictor of how frequently the doctors will be sued for malpractice.[10] Doctors who take the time and effort to deal with the patient's thoughts and feelings get sued less than doctors who don't, regardless of the number and severity of the mistakes the doctors make in diagnosis and treatment.

In the end, clients are loyal if you

1. Get results,
2. Do so efficiently, in both time and cost,

---

6. Charles Dickens, *Bleak House* (1st ed. 1853) (page numbers in the next few footnotes are to the Penguin 1971 edition edited by Norman Page).
7. *Id.* at 52.
8. *Id.* at 145–146.
9. *Id.* at 920–924.
10. Malcolm Gladwell, *Blink: The Power of Thinking Without Thinking* 39–43 (2005).

3. Do none of the things that make people wary of lawyers, and
4. Are considerate, likeably human, and a pleasure to work with in other ways.

Most clients don't want to hire "a lawyer." They want to hire a genuine human being who can use law and other tools to solve and prevent problems.

## §5.5 WORKING WITH TRANSACTIONAL CLIENTS

Get to know the client so you can understand what the client really needs. If the client is a business, get to know the business as well as the industry in which it operates. For example, you can't do good general legal work for a symphony orchestra unless you know things like how grants are obtained from foundations, where the market for classical music recordings is headed, and perhaps what second violinists are typically paid.

How can you learn about your client's business and industry without embarrassing yourself? Read your client's website, books on the industry, and the industry's trade magazines (every industry has at least one). Books on the industry are essential to understanding it in depth. An Internet search can lead you to trade magazine websites and to articles in the general media. Visit the client's place of business to get a feel for it physically and organizationally.

# CHAPTER 6

# INTERVIEWING TRANSACTIONAL CLIENTS

## §6.1 TYPES OF CLIENT INTERVIEWS

The interview is the initial conversation in which the client puts work in the lawyer's hands and the lawyer gets information about the work. In later conversations, usually much shorter ones, the lawyer gets more information from the client. Once you understand how to do the initial interview, those later conversations are easier to accomplish. If later conversations require the client to make decisions, they become counseling, which is covered in Chapters 7 through 11.

*Short-conversation interviewing:* If a transactional client already has a longstanding relationship with you, and if you've worked together on many deals before, you can learn about the transaction in a short conversation, often by telephone. Both lawyer and client can treat this situation as routine.

*Long-conversation interviewing:* An extended conversation, in a face-to-face meeting, is typically needed in two situations: (1) when the lawyer and client have not worked together before and (2) when the client has little or no experience in the type of deal involved. If both of these are true, the conversation will be especially complex.

This chapter concentrates on long-conversation interviewing because it requires many more skills and is harder to learn than short-conversation interviewing. The main skill special to short-conversation interviewing is time-efficiency: getting the most done in the least time. A medium-conversation interview doesn't require unique skills. If you learn how to do long- and short-conversation interviews, you can do anything in between.

## §6.2 SHORT-CONVERSATION CLIENT INTERVIEWING

A term sheet is an informal list, made by the parties, of the business terms they've agreed to (see §1.4). It's usually made while the business people negotiate with each other and before lawyers become involved, although a lawyer might be called in early enough to help create the term sheet. Below is a phone call in which the client tells the lawyer about a deal and asks the lawyer to work on it. Closings are explained in Appendix A.

*Client:* We've just agreed to sell four of our oil tankers to an Italian shipping firm. All of them are on the ocean now, and the buyer will take delivery after they've reached U.S. ports and have off-loaded. I'm sending over the term sheet as an email attachment.

*Lawyer:* When do you want to close?

*Client:* Not until after the last ship is in ballast. They'll be in different ports but we'll close on all of them at the same time. It's all in the term sheet.

*Lawyer:* When do you need the contracts?

*Client:* Yesterday. But early next week is OK.

*Lawyer:* Is the buyer's law firm on the term sheet?

*Client:* Yes.

*Lawyer:* Where can I reach you for questions?

*Client:* Use email if it's simple. If we need to talk, call my cell.

End of conversation. After reading the term sheet and identifying the legal issues, the lawyer will start working on the contract, contacting the buyer's lawyer to negotiate legal issues. This lawyer and client have worked together before. The lawyer knows the client's industry and understands what "off-loaded" and "in ballast" mean.

The lawyer will certainly have further questions for the client. But because this client and lawyer need to use time efficiently, the lawyer will not telephone or email the client every time she has a question. Instead, a lawyer will store up questions, make fewer phone calls and send fewer emails, but ask more questions each time. In the end, the number of questions will be the same. But a busy client will experience each contact as an interruption, and if the same work can be done with fewer interruptions, the client's time is being used more efficiently.

## §6.3 LONG-CONVERSATION CLIENT INTERVIEWING

During long-conversation client interviewing, the lawyer learns about the deal the client has negotiated or is negotiating. Then or later, the lawyer and client also agree on a retainer—the contract through which the client hires the lawyer. Here are the lawyer's purposes in interviewing the client:

*1. To form an attorney–client relationship.* That happens on three levels. One is personal, in that you and the client come to understand each other as people.

To satisfy the client's needs, you need to understand the client as a person and how the problem matters in the client's way of thinking. If you and the client are to work together in the participatory relationship described in Chapter 5, you need to know each other fairly well. And the client can't rely on you without a solid feeling for the person you are. The second level is educational, in that you explain to the client (if the client doesn't already know) things like attorney-client confidentiality and the role the client would or could play in solving the problem. The third is contractual, in that the client agrees to hire you and pay your fees and expenses in exchange for your doing the work you promise to do.

*2. To learn about the transaction.* What are the details? What does the client want the lawyer to do?

*3. To start problem-solving (Chapter 3).* What will the lawyer do after the interview? What will the client do? The lawyer and client need to identify problems and agree on the next steps.

*3. If the client is experiencing stress, to reduce it without being unrealistic.* On a rational level, clients come to lawyers because they want problems solved. But on an emotional level, they might come to get relief from anxiety. Even the client who isn't in a dispute and instead wants something positive done, such as drafting a will, feels a reduction in anxiety when you're able to say—honestly and prudently— "I think we can structure your estate so that almost nothing would be taken in estate taxes and virtually everything would go to your heirs. It would take some work, but I think we can do it." Most of the time, you can't offer even this much assurance in an initial interview because there are too many variables and, at the time of the interview, too many unknowns. Most of the time, clients in initial interviews experience a significant degree of relief from anxiety simply from the knowledge that a capable, concerned, and likeable lawyer is committed to doing whatever is possible to solve the problem. When a client gets that feeling, you're reducing anxiety without being unrealistic.

## §6.4 ORGANIZING THE LONG-CONVERSATION INTERVIEW

You can do a better interview if you prepare beforehand (see §6.5). The interview itself starts with a brief opening in which lawyer and client become acquainted and get down to business (§6.6); continues through an information-gathering phase, the longest part of the interview, in which you learn about the transaction (§§6.7–6.8); and ends with a closing phase in which you and the client agree on what will happen after the interview (§6.9).

## §6.5 PREPARING FOR THE LONG-CONVERSATION INTERVIEW

You might have spoken with the client briefly over the telephone when the client made the appointment. Otherwise, in a well-run office a secretary or a paralegal will have asked the client what kind of work the client is bringing to you. Most of the time, you'll have beforehand at least a vague sense of why the client wants to see you.

Unless you know well the field of law that seems to be involved, take a look at the most obviously relevant parts of the law before the client arrives. If the client wants you to participate in a franchise agreement with McDonald's, for example, look through a practitioner's book or some other source that explains how franchising works in the fast-food industry.

Whoever in your office sets up the client's appointment should ask the client to bring all the papers that are relevant to the transaction.

## §6.6 BEGINNING THE INTERVIEW

In some parts of the country, "visiting"—comfortable chat for a while on topics other than legal work—typically precedes getting down to business. In other regions, no more than two or three sentences might be exchanged first, and they might be limited to questions like whether the client would want some coffee. When it's time to turn to business, the lawyer says something like—

> How can I help? Let's talk about what brings you here today.

And the client might say something like—

> I've inherited an import-export company and want to sell it. I have no idea how to run a business. And my grandchildren will need the money for college and graduate school. How do I handle this? People keep putting pieces of paper in front of me and saying, "Sign here."

Your first instinct will be to ask, "What kind of papers?"—and to exclaim, "Don't sign anything until after I read it and make sure it's OK!"

But wait. Don't leap in immediately. Give the client a full opportunity to tell you whatever he wants to talk about before you start structuring the interview. Many clients want to make sure from the beginning that you hear certain things about which they feel deeply. If you obstruct this, you'll seem remote, even bureaucratic, to the client. And many clients will pour out a torrent of information as soon as you ask them what has brought them into your office. If you listen to this torrent carefully, you may learn a lot of facts in a short period of time. You may also learn a lot about the client as a person and about how the client views the transaction.

Use the client's name during the interview ("Good morning, Ms. Blount"). Saying the client's name at appropriate points in the conversation shortens the psychological distance between you and the client because it implies that you recognize the client as a person rather than as an item of work. Which name you say—the client's first or last name—depends on your personality, your guess about the client's preference, and local customs. If you live in an area where informality is expected, it may be acceptable to call the client by her first name unless the client is so much older than you that, out of respect, you should use the client's last name until the client invites you to switch to first names. But in most parts of the country, the safest practice for a young lawyer is to start on a last-name basis with nearly all clients and wait to see whether you and the client feel comfortable switching to first names.

## §6.7 WHAT TO ASK ABOUT

*The posture of the deal:* What is the present state of discussions between the client and the other party? What has already been agreed to? What issues have not yet been resolved? What obstacles does the client see to wrapping up the agreement? How strongly does the other party want or need this transaction? Is either party in a hurry?

*The details:* List everything the parties have agreed to as well as the issues the parties have not yet resolved. Be sure to get *all* the details. And get them *precisely*. In nonprofessional life, vagueness and approximation are sufficient, and clients often talk in vagueness and approximation. Experienced lawyers know that only precision works.

If the client says, "They're going to pave the access road next month," ask whether the other party has made a commitment to do it next month or has only suggested that it might be able pave next month. And when next month? The middle of the month? The end? What quality of asphalt? Has the other party promised to paint lane-separation lines? Install curbs?

Make sure you learn all the basic information as well: the client's full name; contact information (telephone, email, physical address); and, if the person you're interviewing is the client's employee, that person's job title and responsibilities.

*The parties' goals and interests:* If it's not already obvious, what is each party trying to accomplish in the transaction? Sometimes it's more than just selling or buying something at the best price.

What's the big picture? What about this transaction is most important to the client? To the other party? How will the deal operate financially? Where will the profit be made? How does the client envision the transaction will operate on a practical level once agreement is complete? How does the transaction fit into the client's larger plans for the future? Is the transaction part of a long-term relationship—or a hoped-for long-term relationship—between the parties? What provisions does the client want in the drafted agreement?

*Problems:* What in this deal makes the client anxious? And what worries you as you listen to the client explain the deal? Find out all the facts relevant to the worries.

Every deal is a mixture of opportunity and risk. Clients tend to talk mainly about what they'll get out of the deal (opportunity). You need to protect and, ideally enhance, the opportunities. But you also need to guard against risk.

In drafting the agreement, what potential future difficulties should be provided for in advance? The most obvious example would be breach: How should the agreement define breach, and what consequences would follow breach? Can the transaction be structured to minimize the client's tax? Is there a risk that the transaction might violate the law, particularly a government's administrative regulations? Are there any other ways that the agreement can be drafted to protect the client? In addition, for each type of agreement, there's a laundry list of issues that a prudent lawyer would typically resolve in drafting. (If you rent an apartment, look at your lease; it probably reflects the residential lease version of such a list from the landlord's point of view.) What do you need to know in order to handle the laundry-list issues?

*What does each "supposed to" really mean?* Clients will say that a party is "supposed to do X." When you draft the contract, you'll decide whether that will become a covenant or a condition or both. Many lawyers will instinctively draft it as a covenant, but a covenant alone might not be appropriate. What should happen if the other party doesn't do X? If the consequence should be that the other party will owe your client damages, draft a covenant. If the consequence should be that your client won't be required to do Y, make the other party's doing X a condition to your client's obligation to do Y. If the client would need both consequences, draft a covenant and also draft a promissory condition. (Appendices C and D explain how to sort out these issues.)

*What is the client assuming?* Of the facts the client tells you about, separate the ones the client knows to be true from the ones the client assumes to be true. Often clients aren't consciously aware when something they believe to be true is an unverified assumption. If a fact seems to be important, ask how the client knows about it (unless that's obvious).

If the other party would or should have superior knowledge about a fact your client is assuming, you'll want the other party to represent and warrant the fact in the contract. (This may become a negotiating issue with the other party's lawyer.) You might suggest that your client perform due diligence by investigating and verifying the fact. If you don't obtain a representation and warranty, and your client does no or insufficient due diligence, a court may later hold that your client assumed the risk of ignorance. (Appendix E explains how to sort out these issues.)

*Be fussy.* Ask about *everything*. Charles Fox gives an example:

> A skillful lawyer is adept at sniffing out . . . issues. . . . A client calls up his lawyer and says, "We've just agreed to acquire a used Model 780 pipe threader from Sellco for $3 million. Draw up the papers, but don't spend a lot of time on this."
> 
> The good lawyer will resist the suggestion that he shouldn't take up his or her client's time, and will ask the following questions:
> 
> Is it a *particular* Model 780 (if Sellco has more than one) . . . ?
> Have you examined the equipment and found it satisfactory? . . . [W]hat are the repairs or replacements that need to be made and which party is responsible for making them?
> Who's responsible for moving the equipment from Sellco's plant to yours? . . .

> When is the sale expected to take place? What are . . . the earliest and latest permissible delivery dates? Should either party be able to walk away from the contract if the other side doesn't perform by a specified date? . . .
>
> When does the cash consideration get paid? What form of payment is expected—check or wire transfer? . . . Are you borrowing to pay the purchase price?
>
> . . . Is Sellco willing to warrant its performance for any period of time? Are there existing warranties from the manufacturer . . . ?

This is just the beginning. You would need to continue with many more questions.

## §6.8 SEQUENCING AND FORMULATING QUESTIONS

One of the marks of an effective professional is the ability to ask useful questions in a productive way (see §4.3).

*Organizing questions.* When you start exploring various aspects of the problem in detail, try to take up each topic separately. Too much skipping around confuses you and the client.

With complicated topics, start with broad questions ("Tell me about the difference between a radial engine and an in-line engine") and gradually work your way toward narrow ones ("Why would an aircraft manufacturer use a radial engine when an in-line engine seems more streamlined?"). Broad questions usually produce the largest amount of information, especially information that you haven't anticipated. Narrow questions produce details to fill in gaps left after the broad questions have been asked.

Ask broad questions until you're no longer getting useful information. Then go back and ask narrow questions about the facts the client didn't cover. While the client is answering the broad questions, you can note on a pad the topics you'll explore later with narrow questions.

Move gradually from broad questions to narrow ones. If you jump too quickly to the narrow ones, you'll miss a lot of information because it's the general questions that show you what to explore.

*Formulating questions.* Phrase your questions carefully. Remember that how you say something has an enormous effect on how people respond. A good question doesn't confuse or provoke resistance.

Ask one question at a time, and listen carefully to the answer. If you ask two at a time, only one of them will be answered.

> *Lawyer:* How much did Consolidated bid on this project? Were they the low bidder, or was somebody else?
>
> *Client:* I think somebody else submitted the lowest bid, a company in Milwaukee that later had trouble posting a performance bond.

Did we learn how much Consolidated bid?

## §6.9 ENDING

Assuming that the client wants to hire you and that you want to be hired, two agreements conclude the interview.

One is an agreement that the client is in fact hiring you to do the work discussed in the interview. If the client hasn't made clear that that's happening, ask a simple question like this: "Now that we've talked about it, would you like me to work up a contract and speak with the seller's lawyer?" If you're hired, formalize that through a retainer letter signed by you and countersigned by the client. (This is a contract between you and the client.)

The other agreement concerns what each party will do—and not do—next. Make a realistic and clear commitment of what you'll do in the immediate future, together with a schedule for when you'll do it. Clients feel much better if you set a schedule for accomplishing certain tasks, keep to that schedule, and report back to the client on what you've accomplished. Otherwise, a client has no idea whether you're working diligently or are ignoring the problem.

The client should commit to provide specific things that you need (information, documents) to do your share of the work, and there should be a schedule for this, too. (Paying your retainer is included.)

The end of the interview should provide the client with a sense of closure—a feeling that a problem has been handed over to a professional who will do whatever can be done to solve it. Some clients get closure from the mutual agreements described above. Others may appreciate a comment from you that shows that you understand what this problem means for the client and are concerned about it on a human level.

Explain to the client how best to contact you. That is most easily done by giving the client your business card, which will include your phone number and your email address. You might explain your habits in returning phone calls. For example, if you tend to return client phone calls late in the day, explain that to the client and add that if the client needs a faster response she should say when leaving a message that the subject is urgent.

# PART III

# COUNSELING AND ADVICE

# CHAPTER 7

# COUNSELING AND ADVISING TRANSACTIONAL CLIENTS

## §7.1 THE DIFFERENCE BETWEEN COUNSELING AND ADVICE

*Advising* is explaining to a client how the law treats the client's situation. Counseling is guiding a client through the process of making a decision.[1] Lawyers don't always recognize this distinction. They may use the words *advice* and *counseling* interchangeably, as synonyms. But advising and counseling are separate skills, and you'll learn them more deeply if you distinguish between them.

It's possible to advise without counseling. A client calls you and asks, "Will I pay more tax if I do X in New York than if I do it in the Cayman Islands?" You tell the client what the tax will be in New York and what it will be in the Cayman Islands and why and how the tax will be different. The client hangs up. Regardless of what the client does next, you've only provided advice by explaining how the law treats the client's situation.

This client asked a narrow question and just wanted to know how much something would cost (tax). That's not different from calling up a supplier and asking, "How much will I pay for 200 gizmos delivered next Thursday?" In each situation, the client will factor the cost into a business decision, and neither you nor the supplier will participate in that decision, even though you've both provided necessary information. (By the way, the client might decide to do X in New York because the Cayman Islands tax advantage is outweighed by other business

---

1. David A. Binder & Susan C. Price, *Legal Interviewing and Counseling: A Client-Centered Approach* 5 (1977).

considerations. But the client would not be able to make that decision without knowing what taxes would cost in both places.)

Counseling includes advice, but it's much more as well. To guide a client through making a decision, a lawyer develops options, estimates their advantages and disadvantages, and helps the client choose the option that would most effectively help achieve the client's goals. In the course of doing that, the lawyer would have to explain how the law will treat the client's situation. The client treated the New York-or-Cayman Islands question as a business decision. You didn't participate in making it because you know less about making business decisions than this client does. In fact, you might not even understand the business issues. A lawyer will counsel—help to structure the decision—when the client realizes that the legal issues are more complex and might dominate the decision.

Counseling has two parts. The first, preparation, includes identifying the client's goals and developing alternative potential solutions that, to varying degrees, might accomplish those goals. (Chapter 9 explains how.) The second is a discussion with the client in which the lawyer explains the options so the client can choose between or among them. Relatively simple decisions without emotional content can be handled in a phone conversation. If a decision is more complex or would affect the client emotionally, a face-to-face meeting might be necessary. (Chapter 10 explains how to conduct those discussions.)

Effective counselors combine empathy and detachment, two things that don't naturally exist side by side. Empathy helps you understand the client's goals and needs (see §4.4). Detachment helps you see the problem as it really is, without delusion. "The wise counselor is one who is able to see his client's situation from within and yet, at the same time, from a distance, and thus to give advice that is at once compassionate and objective."[2]

## §7.2 "DECISION-MAKING IS AN ART"[3]

A well-made decision of any kind is a product of professional problem-solving operating through the six steps laid out in Chapter 3. In client counseling those steps are

1. Identifying the problem about which the client must make a decision
2. Gathering and evaluating information and raw materials to be used in making that decision
3. Generating potential solutions to the problem, as options from which the client can choose
4. Evaluating each option to measure its advantages, costs, risks, and odds of success
5. Helping the client choose an option
6. Acting on that choice

---

2. Anthony Kronman, *Living in the Law*, 54 U. Chi. L. Rev. 835, 866 (1987).
3. Warren Lehman, *The Pursuit of a Client's Interest*, 77 Mich. L. Rev. 1078, 1094 (1979).

You'll become better at this as you develop an effective problem-solving style and learn the thinking described in Chapter 3.

Ask yourself what *practical* problems you see as a disinterested observer. This doesn't necessarily have anything to do with law, but it's among the most valuable things a lawyer can provide for a client. A lawyer who confines herself to legal questions is a technician. A lawyer who also goes beyond the legal questions is a problem-solver.

## §7.3 TWO CHALLENGES IN COUNSELING

*Creating options:* It's not enough just to identify options that are immediately obvious from applying law to facts. *Create* options that wouldn't be there except for your insights and problem-solving skills. And the options should go beyond law: They should be practical solutions that will work in the real world where the client lives, not just in law books.

*Working out each option precisely:* Precisely define the value of an option—especially where the value can be stated in numbers and with certainty. The following doesn't help the client.

> If you choose the fourth option, you'll receive $219,000, and you'll have to pay tax on it.

Here's what the client really needs to know:

> If you choose the fourth option, you'll receive $219,000 within 30 days, on which you'll owe tax of 35% or $76,650, so you'll get to keep $142,350. This option is really worth $142,350 to you. That's what you'd get to keep.

## §7.4 WHY SOME CLIENTS EXCLUDE THEIR LAWYERS FROM IMPORTANT DECISIONS

Lani Guinier tells the following story about a construction company, Bovis General Contractors, and an office building:

> Before beginning construction, but after the contracts were formally negotiated by the lawyers, a team from Bovis arranged a meeting attended by the [future] owners of the building, the architects, the engineers, and those who would be using the building. The Bovis team encouraged those present to identify important issues at the outset. Everyone agreed they wanted the project to come in on time and under budget; to meet the needs of the building's users; and to lead to long-term relationships with each of the other parties.
>
> Most poignant is that these business people *did not invite lawyers* to their meeting. The lawyers negotiated the contract under which everyone was operating, but the [meeting] participants negotiated duties without ever referring to or consulting [that]

contract.... The lawyers' approach, which is understandably based on avoiding client [liability] in the event things go awry, often forecloses the *human interaction*—the pleasant exchanges and gestures—*which assure that things go right.* Indeed, *Bovis boasts that it has never had a lawsuit filed when it leaves lawyers out of the room and negotiates interpersonal agreements among the participants themselves.*[4]

Some clients believe that lawyers listen too little, dominate conversations, poison relationships by generating conflict, and raise objections when they should be developing solutions. Business people call this kind of lawyer a "deal killer"—a lawyer who can sabotage a deal the client really wants.

*Another example:* The Ebola virus usually leads to death after horrible suffering. In the earliest-known outbreaks, 89% of the people infected in the Congo died, as did 53% of those infected in the Sudan. Like many diseases, Ebola can spread from other primates to humans. For that reason, monkeys imported into the United States must be kept in temporary quarantine to make sure that they aren't bringing infectious diseases into the country. In the late 1980s, monkeys in one quarantine facility had become infected with Ebola. This building was in a small industrial park adjacent to an elementary school near residential neighborhoods in Reston, Virginia, a suburb of Washington, D.C.

The U.S. Army Medical Research Institute of Infectious Diseases (USAMRIID) was responsible for developing defenses against biological weapons that might be used by terrorists or by an enemy in war. If the United States were attacked with biological weapons, USAMRIID would have been expected to send biohazard SWAT teams immediately to limit infection and treat victims. Although the monkey infections were a naturally occurring outbreak and not an attack, the owner of the quarantine facility invited USAMRIID to take over the building, set up bio-containment barriers to keep Ebola from spreading outside the facility, kill the infected monkeys, and decontaminate the building. No statute gives the Army the authority to do this when the country is not being attacked, and if the Army accidentally spread Ebola to the surrounding area, the potential legal liabilities could be enormous. To prevent public panic, USAMRIID decided to send its team in secret, using rented civilian trucks and without telling anyone nearby—including officials at the elementary school—what they were doing.

Before beginning this operation, USAMRIID consulted an Army general in the Pentagon. No lawyer was present during this conversation.

> Was this legal? Could the Army simply put together a biohazard SWAT team and move in on the monkey house? General Russell was afraid that the Army's lawyers would tell him that it could not, and should not, be done, so he answered the legal doubts with these words: "A policy of moving out and doing it, and asking forgiveness afterward, is better than a policy of asking permission and having it denied. *You never ask a lawyer for permission to do something. We are going to do the needful, and [afterward] the lawyers are going to tell us why it's legal.*"[5]

---

4. Lani Guinier, *Lessons and Challenges of Becoming Gentlemen*, 24 N.Y.U. Rev. of L. & Soc. Change 1, 13–14 (1998) (italics added).
5. Richard Preston, *The Hot Zone* 159 (1994) (italics added).

Fortunately, no human became ill. (Scientists later discovered that this strain of Ebola—now called Ebola-Reston—does not make humans ill as other strains do.)

What could General Russell have been afraid of? Like the business people discussed earlier, he probably had had bad experiences with lawyers who raise objections in a single-minded effort to reduce legal risks, even if the client is willing to take those risks to achieve an important goal. Why do some lawyers behave this way? Here are some possibilities:

Some lawyers think bureaucratically, dividing everything into what's legal and what's illegal, even though a large gray area, where the law is unclear, exists between the plainly legal and the plainly illegal. An early twentieth-century lawyer named Elihu Root is often cited for the statement that most of the practice of law is telling clients that they are acting like fools and should stop. There is some truth in that, and a wise lawyer knows how to deliver that kind of advice in a way the client can accept.

But perhaps a more important quote is this: "I don't want a lawyer to tell me what I cannot do; I hire him to tell me *how* to do what I want to do." That quote has an unattractive reputation because of the person who said it—J. P. Morgan, a robber-baron financier who was a contemporary of Root. But stripped of that association, it states what all clients want from their lawyers—not just the rich and powerful but also the family that runs a neighborhood bodega and wants to incorporate, or the political refugee who seeks asylum here to escape persecution in his own country. They all want a lawyer who can show them how to accomplish their goals and help them do so.

Business people tend to believe that some lawyers raise objections rather than solve problems, and those lawyers are viewed as obstructionists and deal killers. A substantial business can replace that kind of lawyer with one who has better problem-solving skills. But the family with the bodega will probably feel that the first lawyer they consult is giving them the answer that all lawyers would give. Some business people say that when confronted with an idea that has some faults, the bureaucratic mind will reject it to avoid risk while the entrepreneurial mind will find a way to improve it to create an opportunity. They want their lawyers to think like entrepreneurs rather than bureaucrats.

Most of law school teaches how to read cases and statutes, but not necessarily how to solve problems. Law school also emphasizes shooting down ideas, which can give the impression that that is the heart of what lawyers are paid to do. But shooting down every imperfect idea makes a lawyer a destructive presence rather than a constructive one. A lawyer's job is to *find or create solutions*.

Sometimes the only realistic answer is no. The law explicitly prohibits what the client wants to do, and for decades, every attempted strategy to get around that prohibition has failed. But that's unusual. More often, the law might not permit the exact thing the client wants, but the client's *interests* might be advanced in some way by looking at the situation in a different way and defining the client's goal differently. Say no only when truly there are no viable solutions.

In addition, some lawyers, especially inexperienced ones, don't know when or how to take risks, even necessary ones. Business people can't make money without taking risks, and the most effective business people are skilled at separating profitable risks from pointless ones. People at the top of large organizations (such as generals) sometimes can feel the same way, even where profit is not an issue (as in the Army), because they can see the bigger picture and more readily balance need against risk.

If General Russell had called in the Army's lawyers, what would have been good counseling? The lawyer should make sure that the clients—the general and the people from USAMRIID—understand the potential for liability, and she should brainstorm with them ways to minimize the legal risks. She should also brainstorm ways to minimize public hostility if the operation is less than fully successful. For example, from both a liability and a public relations standpoint, conducting this operation in secret, using disguised vehicles, while an elementary school is in session nearby, seems like an unnecessary risk. A monkey that escapes during the operation could get onto the school grounds and infect children. But that should not cause the lawyer to say no. Instead, she should help work out a way of achieving client goals while reducing legal risks. A good problem-solving lawyer might explore the possibility of enlisting the highest officials in the school district as collaborators, if they will be both decisive and discreet, and closing the school on a pretext (some reason other than Ebola, even if it's a ruse) to avoid public panic.

# CHAPTER 8

# SOME EXAMPLES OF COUNSELING AND ADVICE

## §8.1 ADVICE

*Answering a narrow question from the client, often over the telephone.* A lawyer sits in her office writing or reading. The phone rings, and she picks it up. A client asks, "Can we legally sell tractors to the Cuban government?" When answering, the lawyer isn't counseling because her role isn't to structure a decision. The client just wants to know how the law would treat this transaction.

The lawyer is giving advice, and there's a technique to it. Give the bottom-line answer (yes or no). Explain why. If a change in the facts might change the answer, explain that, especially if the client can change the facts ("If you sell to a Canadian company that trades with Cuba . . ."). If the law has gaps or uncertainties, explain them. Don't answer until you're confident that you know exactly what the law is, and if that involves delay, estimate how long the delay will be ("I want to check a few things, and I'll get back to you later this morning"). Make a written note of the advice you give, and keep those notes in the client's file in case of a misunderstanding later about what you said or why you said it.

*Participation in business planning.* This might happen in a meeting in which the lawyer is only one of several people in the room. Depending on the situation, the lawyer might figuratively sit on the sidelines, interjecting advice about legal concerns as they become relevant. But the business people are structuring their own decisions because the business issues predominate. The lawyer is there as a resource.

## §8.2 COUNSELING

*Answering a broad question from the client.* Again the phone rings, and the lawyer answers it. A long-standing client asks a broad question: "Do you see any problems with the letter of intent in the Icelandic Hydro deal?" If the answer is "no," it's close to advice. But the lawyer's answer might be more complicated:

> I see two problems. X can be fixed when we do the contract. They'll cooperate because it's a problem for them as well. Their lawyer will want to haggle over it, but I'm not worried.
>
> The other problem is Y, and it's much harder. As the deal is structured, you could run into some potential legal liability. *[The lawyer explains how.]* It's not certain that you'd be liable, but there's a serious risk. *[She estimates the odds.]* This isn't the sort of thing that can be solved when I draft the contract. It's inherent in the deal itself. *[Explains why.]*
>
> You might want to renegotiate the price to compensate you for the risk. If you want, I can write a letter to you explaining the liability risk so you can show it to them. But if you show them a letter from me explaining the liability risk, that might cause future problems for you if they refuse and you go through with the deal anyway. *[Explains why.]* If they won't renegotiate price, you'd have to decide whether this deal is worth the liability risk or whether you should walk away from it. *[Explains more.]*

Here the lawyer is counseling because she's explaining the Y problem, laying out some options for dealing with it, and explaining the advantages and disadvantages of the options. She's structuring a decision and giving the client a roadmap for deciding.

If you're the lawyer, take careful written notes of what the client is saying. Before answering, make sure you understand the facts. Summarize them as you think you have heard them and ask the person at the other end of the line whether you've got them right ("Let me make sure I've got the facts right . . ."). Don't answer the other person's questions until you're confident that you know exactly what the law is, and if that involves delay, estimate how long the delay will be. Make written notes of what the client told you and what you told the client. And sometimes consider writing a letter or email to the client memorializing what you heard and what you said.

*Counseling complicated enough to need a face-to-face meeting.* The Icelandic Hydro problem can probably be handled over the telephone if the lawyer and client already have a relationship, the issue is straightforward, the options are few, and it's a pure business decision without emotional content. It might take several phone conversations to cover everything, and not just the one described above. But a face-to-face meeting might be needed if the negative dollar value of the risk would require a lot of explanation, if several of the client's employees would need to hear what the lawyer has to say, or if one or more of the client's decision-makers are skeptical about what the lawyer is saying.

*Counseling during the contract-formation stage.* The client and another company have talked about how each could earn some money buying or selling something to the other. They've already agreed to some of the business terms—price, quantity, delivery dates, and so forth. You haven't been part of these discussions. At a point when the deal seems to be jelling, the client calls you and asks that you "reduce it to writing" (produce a written contract, which will govern the transaction).

After you and the client talk things over, you rough-draft a contract. This isn't the final version. After you and the client review the draft, you rewrite it and send it to the other company's lawyer. (Or if that lawyer has already written a draft, you rewrite it.) Negotiations between the lawyers ensue. Afterward, you rewrite the agreement again to reflect the results of the negotiations.

Sometimes this lawyer-to-lawyer negotiation resolves all the issues the lawyers identify. But often it doesn't, and you might need to ask your client to make decisions. At some point, or at a number of points, you and the client might have conversations in which you frame alternative ways of solving problems and estimate each alternative's effectiveness.

## §8.3 COUNSELING ON A VERY LARGE SCALE (THE PLANT CLOSING)

You've been hired by a labor union that represents the 432 employees of a local manufacturing plant. They were told last week that the plant will close 21 days later (two weeks from today) because the huge corporation that owns it is no longer satisfied with the modest profit earned by the product the employees make, and also because the corporation has been unable to persuade anybody else to buy and operate the plant. The corporation wants to concentrate its efforts only in product lines where the profits are spectacular. The employees want to continue working in this plant. They have families to support and are unlikely to find equivalent work in the local economy. The corporation says that such things are not relevant to bottom lines on corporate balance sheets, and that the employees' paychecks will end on the day the plant closes.

## §8.3.1 PREPARING TO COUNSEL THE EMPLOYEES

*Identifying the union's goals.* The union members want to keep their jobs. You have spoken with many of them individually, and it seems that, aside from the obvious and paramount need to preserve income, the workers want these jobs for three reasons: (1) most of them have worked in this plant for years, know each other, and feel a sense of community that they don't want to lose; (2) most of them are in middle or late-middle age and fear that they won't be able to find equivalent work elsewhere or adapt to it if it is available; and (3) many of them say that the work, although hard, is satisfying. (It would have been easy for you to just take the union's goal as "save jobs," but you learned so much more when you looked beyond that.) The workers aren't interested in revenge. And although they think it would be nice if the world were to operate so that this kind of thing didn't happen, they aren't out to change the world.

*Gathering and evaluating relevant information about both the law and the facts.* You check the law and find the following:

Your state is one of the few with a plant-closing statute, and it might be the strongest statute in the country. It requires employers to give 120 days notice to employees before permanently closing an employment site at which the workforce has exceeded 250 people at any time during the preceding 24 months. An employer who does not do so is liable to affected employees for triple the wages not paid between the time the plant does close and a date that occurs 120 days after notice is given. Nothing in the statute requires an employer to pay employees after the 120-day notice expires, and nothing requires the employer actually to operate the plant during the 120 days. This statute is relatively new. Business groups claim that it violates the interstate commerce clause of the federal constitution as well as the due process and equal protection clauses of the Fourteenth Amendment. No court in your state has ruled on the question, but in other states courts have upheld weaker plant closing statutes against similar challenges.

The federal Worker Adjustment and Retraining Notification Act (WARN) requires notification 60 days before a plant closing. There are big exceptions, but these facts are not within them. The penalty for violations is much softer than under your state's statute. An employer who violates both statutes pays only the larger penalty (not both).

Nothing else in state or federal law requires an employer to give employees any severance payments of any kind.

The federal Consolidated Omnibus Budget Reconciliation Act of 1985 (COBRA) provides that—under the circumstances that exist here—an employer must arrange for discharged employees to continue their health insurance coverage temporarily, but at the employees' own expense. Insurance through COBRA has two advantages. First, it can be, but is not always, cheaper than insurance bought on the open market. Second, because it's a continuation of, rather than new, insurance, employees with chronic illnesses, which the insurance industry calls "preexisting conditions," will not be discriminated against.

Your state's unemployment compensation plan will pay the equivalent of one-third of each employee's wages for 26 weeks after they cease to be employed.

Some lawyers would stop here on the idea that lawyers apply law to facts and don't do much else. But you know that lawyers are problem-solvers and not mere technicians, so you go further and find out the following:

The land on which the plant sits is zoned only for industrial use and is surrounded for some distance in every direction by similar land. Some other neighboring plants have also closed within the past few years, and several of them are now dilapidated shells. There are few buyers for this kind of real estate locally. Most of the dilapidated factories are still owned by the companies that once operated them, and these companies continue to pay property taxes on them. A few are now owned by the local government because bids at tax foreclosure sales were insufficient.

Most of the equipment in the plant will be serviceable for at least a decade. It's not new, but it is not obsolete either. The manufacturing process is labor-intensive. That means that although the equipment is essential, there is not much of it in the factory. There is a market for used equipment of this kind, but it's erratic. That means that if the corporation tried to sell the equipment, it might find a buyer right away or never.

The product manufactured in the plant is bought by other businesses for use in their own work. It's the kind of product that one buys continually rather than only once in a while. Because the brand made in this factory is known for its high quality, many customers habitually buy it rather than competing brands. But profits in manufacturing this product will never be more than modest because customers will not pay more than a certain price for it, no matter how good it is.

None of the workers has any significant savings. All are blue collar, and many are literally the working poor. None has any managerial experience or knows anything about finance or marketing.

The corporation is exclusively profit-minded. It does whatever earns or saves money. It operates no other plant in this state.

Visiting the plant and using a telephone, a law library, and the Internet, a lawyer would probably need between 12 and 20 hours of work to collect all this information.

*Generating potential solutions.* You come up with the following list. (These are not alternatives. The union could decide to do more than one of them.)

1. Take action to get the corporation to obey the state's plant closing statute.
2. Advise the workers of their COBRA rights and give them the information they would need to file unemployment compensation claims.
3. Organize protests, lobbying efforts, and media exposure to persuade Congress, the state legislature, or both to adopt remedial legislation.
4. Find a way for the workers to buy the plant and keep on manufacturing the product.

*Evaluating potential solutions.* When you tally up the advantages, costs, risks, and chances of success for each of these options, this is what you get:

1. *Action under the plant closing statutes.* Under the state statute, this would get the workers an additional 99 days of income but would accomplish nothing else. The corporation's obligation is clear under the statute. Although there's a possibility that the corporation might be able to get the statute held unconstitutional, that seems unlikely, given the case law. And the corporation is unlikely to try. It has little motivation because it owns no other plant in the state, might be accruing triple penalties while challenging the statute, and, even if the state statute were struck down, the federal statute would still impose some penalties, although they would be weaker. The chances of success here are high. A prudent lawyer doesn't promise that a particular result is 100% certain: facts that you don't yet know about might defeat a client's claim. The cost to the union would be anywhere from your hourly rate for a few hours of work (if the corporation voluntarily agrees to obey the statute) to a very high sum (if the corporation challenges the statute in court). You predict that the cost will be toward the low end of that scale, although the corporation won't agree easily.

2. *Advising the workers of their COBRA and unemployment compensation rights.* The workers qualify for COBRA and unemployment compensation, both of which are better than nothing. But that, too, doesn't accomplish the union's goals. Unemployment compensation is not a job, let alone the job each worker now has; it is temporary; and it will provide less money than a paycheck would. The unemployment benefits for these workers might be so low that they might not be able to afford COBRA insurance. Although the value of this option is low, the cost of obtaining it is also low. It would take you no more than a few hours to make sure that all the workers are fully informed of what they're entitled to and how to get it.

3. *Lobbying, etc.* The state already has the strongest plant closing statute in the country. You might be able to imagine other legislation, but it would not be applied retroactively to these workers. Although legislation applied prospectively might improve society, this option does nothing to advance the goals of the workers, who are worried about their families.

4. *Buying the plant.* If it were possible, this option would satisfy nearly all the union's goals and also give the workers more control over their lives than they have had as employees. It would require capital to buy the plant; managerial, financial, and marketing expertise to keep it going and sell the product; and a transition plan that would maintain the existing market for the product, keep raw materials coming in, and keep the new worker-owners from being overwhelmed immediately by snafus and operating expenses.

Taken together, that seems impossible. But you break it down into its parts:

The plant and its equipment will not easily find any other ready buyer, and if the corporation doesn't sell the real estate soon, it will have to continue to pay property taxes on it. You have already established that the corporation owes each worker 99 days more wages than the corporation thought it did. This is not a huge expense for a giant corporation, but you have increased the cost to the corporation of closing the factory. And you might be able to show the company that it would be cheaper to help the workers buy the place.

An operating plant pumps money into a local economy that a closed plant does not. From the local government's point of view, it might be a good investment to give the new worker-owners, all local voters, a rebate on the plant's property taxes to help get the plant established in their hands.

If, on the other hand, the corporation continues to own the plant, it will still owe property taxes even though the plant would produce no revenue. To avoid this expense, which will recur every year indefinitely, the corporation might save money by selling the plant to the employees now at a discounted price or by lending the employees the money they would need to buy the plant. And even though the corporation might do that to save money, it could portray the sale for public relations purposes as an act of generosity by a responsible corporate citizen. You have seen many advertisements in which companies bragged about things they have done for communities or the environment so the public will feel better buying the companies' products. You wonder whether the opportunity to do this is an asset to which corporations and their accountants can assign a dollar value. And you wonder whether this corporation cares enough about public relations to consider selling to the employees to be a good investment.

Some corporations wouldn't see it that way. And some corporations would eliminate their property taxes on hard-to-sell land simply by no longer paying them and waiting for the local government to seize the property to pay off the tax deficiency. But that would take the property off the tax rolls because the local government wouldn't be able to sell it, in addition to the local unemployment that would be generated when the plant closes. If the corporation takes this approach, we're taken back to the local government as a potential source of assistance for the employees. These two results—a reduction in property tax revenue and an increase in unemployment—can damage the government's budget and the local economy, which gives the local government an incentive to help.

You see the germ of something here, although you also see problems. Things can get harsher when workers own the business. For example, it's always true that some employees are less efficient than others. Will the more efficient employees resent the less efficient ones when profitability affects everybody's income? Right now, this is at best an incomplete option. You haven't been able to create a plan that would make it work. For that reason, you aren't yet in a position to estimate costs for this option.

## §8.3.2 MEETING WITH THE STEERING COMMITTEE

This is an unusual counseling session because you're meeting not with one or two people, but with the nine representatives that the union members have elected as their steering committee to address this problem. You begin by stating your understanding of the union's goals so that if your understanding is wrong, it will be corrected. You then describe some of the facts that you consider especially important: the difficulty the corporation will have selling the plant and equipment, the loyalty of the plant's customers, the reputation of its product, and so on.

You say that you have thought of four options, but before you list them you would like to ask the committee just to listen to you, without leaping to judgment. You will list all the choices and then describe how each would work and its advantages, costs, risks, and chances of success. You add that three of the options will sound inadequate and the fourth will sound impossible, but you ask for patience because you think that you and the steering committee might be able to brainstorm the fourth option into something the union might find acceptable.

You then list the options, and body language tells you that the group is not pleased. "You mean there's nothing in the law," someone asks, "that says they have to keep this plant open as long as we're making a profit for them?" You say, "No," but this question makes you realize that if the workers buy the plant, they don't have to make any profit at all. If they borrow money to buy the plant, all profit, or what used to be profit, can go to debt repayment.

You then go through the options one by one, describing their advantages, costs, risks, and chances of success. You present the last option (buying the plant) as an incomplete idea and point to the problems: The workers would need to hire managers and financial and marketing people. It would be awkward because hired managers would be supervising the owners of the business. And where would the money come from to buy the plant?

"I've worked for this company for 37 years," says one of the steering committee members, "and in the last five or six years they did nothing to make this plant work. They didn't like the product and treated it like a stepchild. They sent us dumb managers who belong in a Dilbert cartoon, probably rejects from other factories. We made this place work, and now they throw us out in the street!"

"I know of a manager who doesn't belong in a Dilbert cartoon," says someone else. "Isaiah Joyner's daughter got a college degree in business, works in some high-stress job in a big city, and hates it. Think she'd like to come back here?"

This meeting goes on for a long time. At the end, the steering committee votes to make a conditional recommendation to the union membership that they negotiate with the corporation to buy the plant, using the severance that the corporation would otherwise have to pay as part of the purchase price and borrowing the rest from the corporation itself or elsewhere.

There are two conditions. One is that a business plan be developed first, demonstrating that the workers could buy and operate the plant while retaining its customers. The other condition is that the county and municipal governments commit themselves to rebate most of the property taxes for several years if the workers buy the plant.

The steering committee also votes that if these conditions aren't met, the recommendation to the union membership will be to get what they're entitled to under the state plant closing statute, COBRA, and unemployment compensation and start looking for other jobs.

The business plan would have to be developed very quickly because not much time is left before the corporation otherwise will close the plant. The next morning you pick up the phone to call Isaiah Joyner's daughter. As you dial, you hope that she's very capable, has time to spare right now, can help you estimate the costs of the buyout option and its chances of success, and would like to come back to live in your community.

# CHAPTER 9

# PREPARING FOR COUNSELING: STRUCTURING THE OPTIONS

## §9.1 FOCUSING ON CLIENT GOALS AND PREFERENCES

*Client goals.* Get clear answers to these questions: "What do you [the client] want to gain out of this transaction? What should we try to make sure that you get? How does this transaction fit into your overall plans for the future?"

Don't assume you know the client's goals. Two clients who want the same kind of transaction might want it for very different reasons and therefore have very different goals. A client whom you helped to buy land last week might have wanted it to preserve wilderness (you might have represented the Nature Conservancy). Another client whom you're helping to buy a different plot of land this week might want it for reasons that would have the opposite effect (you might be representing a shopping center developer).

Virtually all transactional clients will need to minimize any legal liability or taxes that might grow out of the transaction. But they might not realize these are issues until you point that out.

*Client preferences.* A goal is what the client hired you to get. A preference is something the client would like you to do or not do while pursuing goals. "Don't play hardball on this" is a preference. The client wants you to accomplish something but has instructed you not to use hardball tactics to get it, perhaps because the client doesn't want to risk killing the deal or harming a long-term relationship with the other party.

Client preferences are important because they will affect each potential solution's value to the client. You need to know not only the preferences, but also how intense they are. There's a big difference between "If you can avoid it . . ." and "Under no circumstances . . ." Find out why the preference exists. One client might prefer to get money soon because, once invested, early money earns more in interest, dividends, and capital gains than late money does. Another client might prefer to get money soon to pay mounting medical bills.

For many clients, the most important preference is represented by their tolerance or intolerance for risk (see §9.4).

## §9.2 DEVELOPING OPTIONS (POTENTIAL SOLUTIONS)

Notice that the solution developed in §8.3.1 (buying the factory) didn't leap out of Lexis or Westlaw. The lawyer created it by combining a number of raw ingredients. Some of the ingredients came from the law, and others came from the lawyer's good judgment and understanding of the people involved and the business practicalities of the situation.

Don't just list the obvious solutions ("the law will let you do X, but it won't let you do Y"). Find ways to *create* solutions. That's what clients believe they're paying you to do. Chapter 3 explains how. Don't limit yourself to how the law will treat the client. Think in bigger terms. Consider the people involved and their needs. If money is at issue, think about the wisest way to deal with it, taking into account all the costs and the way the relevant markets and financial institutions operate. Think in practical terms. Inclusive solutions (§3.5) are often the most long-lasting and satisfying ones.

## §9.3 PREDICTING WHAT EACH OPTION WOULD CAUSE

Ben Franklin said that complicated decisions are hard to make because

> all the reasons pro and con are not present in the mind at the same time; but sometimes one set present themselves, and at other times another, the first being out of sight . . . [and] uncertainty . . . perplexes us.
>
> To get over this, my way is to divide half a sheet of paper by a line into two columns; writing over the one Pro, and over the other Con. Then . . . I [write] down under the different head[ing]s short hints of the different motives, that at different times occur to me, for or against the measure. When I have thus got them all together in one view, I endeavor to estimate their respective weights . . . and thus proceeding I find at length where the balance lies. . . .
>
> And, though the weight of reasons cannot be taken with the precision of algebraic quantities . . . when each is thus considered, separately and comparatively, and the whole lies before me, I think I can judge better, and am less likely to take a rash step. . . .[1]

---

1. Letter from Franklin to Joseph Priestley, from *The Benjamin Franklin Sampler* (1956) (spelling and capitalization have been modernized).

This is solution-evaluation as explained in §3.2. Estimate—in detail—the advantages, costs, risks, and chances of success of each option. That requires you to make predictions. You can express a prediction either in descriptive phrases (such as "a good chance of success" or "highly likely") or in numbers ("odds of about two out of three" or "a 50/50 chance of success"). Both methods have problems.

Descriptive phrases might be too vague to be meaningful to the client, or even to you. An optimistic client might hear "the chances are good" to mean "we are definitely going to accomplish this." How much probability do we have when there's "an excellent chance of success"? A client making an important decision might want a more meaningful measure of probability.

On the other hand, numbers can imply a precision that isn't really there. Predictive estimates are by nature inexact, and a prediction that something is 65% likely to happen isn't significantly different from a prediction that it's 60% or 70% likely—although a client could easily think otherwise because you're using exact numbers. Avoid predicting in percentage terms and instead limit yourself to more general statements expressed in fractions, such as "odds of three in four."

Predicting can be frightening. How can you possibly assure a client that you know exactly what the future will bring? You can't, but you have to predict anyway. It might help to remember that every day billions of dollars are invested, lent, or otherwise committed based on predictions of whether customers will like a product or hate it, whether stock prices or interest rates will rise or fall, whether Congress will do this or that, or even whether there will be lots of rain or only a little over the next few months in the wheat belt or the corn belt or some other place where crops are grown. Many of those predictions turn out to be wrong. The earth won't swallow you up if a prediction you make turns out to be inaccurate. But professionals whose predictions mostly tend to be right gain the loyalty and respect of their clients, both in investing and in law.

Out of fear of being wrong, you might want to hedge, which could be either bad or good. One form of hedging—waffling—makes your advice less useful to a client, who must make a decision and needs the best prediction you're capable of. From the client's point of view if you waffle, you aren't really predicting. Another form of hedging—adding qualifications or conditions—can make your prediction *more* precise because qualifications and conditions identify variables that might change your prediction ("we stand less than a 50/50 chance of getting the zoning board to approve this unless we can show that the neighbors won't be affected").

Often, you'll have to predict without complete knowledge of the facts or the law. Some facts might not become available to you until later, or only at some expense, or never. And some parts of the law are unsettled. When you predict, identify not only what you know, but also what you don't know. And where you notice a gap in your knowledge, define exactly how the gap would influence the prediction and estimate how and when that gap can be filled and how much it would cost to do so. (Sometimes the cost of filling the gap will exceed the value to be gained in making the prediction more accurate.)

Your predictions should be frank and disinterested. If there's bad news, the client needs to know it. Hiding it from the client does neither her nor you a favor (and it risks the kind of misunderstanding that can turn into an ethics complaint or a malpractice action).

You should be able to articulate a reason for each prediction. When you talk with the client, you'll need to explain that reason. And if you force yourself to articulate it now, while preparing, your predictions will be more accurate because the act of articulating will force you to bring your unconscious thinking out in the open where you can see its gaps and inconsistencies.

Finally, consider the moral dimension. We're too used to assuming that when people act in their own self-interest, they'll act selfishly. In a world where material success and conspicuous consumption are so important, people are led to believe that in many situations, especially where lawyers are involved, maximizing their own gain is what they're *supposed* to do. But for more clients than you might suppose, doing the morally right thing can be in their own self-interest. Being fair, or even generous, can help them feel better about themselves and build a valuable reputation as well as valuable relationships with others (see §11.1).

## §9.4 ADAPTING TO THE CLIENT'S TOLERANCE FOR RISK

Many people will easily bet small amounts of money—$5 on a lottery ticket or $25 on the office World Series or Super Bowl pool. Some people won't bet at all; they have no taste for it, or it violates their convictions. Some people feel comfortable staking relatively large bets, such as $1,000 in a poker game. And some people bet with money they cannot afford to lose.

If you think of gambling as limited to lotteries, office pools, poker, and the like, you'll probably say that you don't gamble often or that you never gamble. But every time you make a decision based on a prediction of the future, you're gambling. You gamble every day, in fact, in small ways. If it takes you 30 minutes to drive to school and if your first class of the day is with a teacher who won't tolerate tardiness, you're gambling that you'll have no trouble finding a parking space when you leave home 25 minutes before class.

We win a lot of the small gambles of everyday life, but we also lose a lot of them. In the end, it doesn't matter much because both the benefits of winning and the costs of losing are not terribly great. You're embarrassed if you walk into class late, and the embarrassment might cause you to stop making that particular gamble. But you still have your family and friends, your net worth is unchanged, and you haven't added significantly to the amount of injustice in the world. Even if you win, what have you won? Maybe an extra five minutes at home.

The big gambles are much more frightening. Tolerance for risk decreases as the stakes get bigger. A person who casually bets $20 on a horse race might be a lot more hesitant if three zeros were added to that amount. And the size of the stake is always relative. To some people with very large financial resources, even a $20,000 bet is not significant enough to cause anxiety. And to others in precarious circumstances, $20 can be a lot of money.

Whatever the client's tolerance for risk, it's entitled to your respect. The client, after all, must live with the consequences of the decision long after you've disappeared from the client's life. You do, however, have an obligation to point out the disadvantages of betting to clients with high tolerances for risk and the disadvantages of not betting to clients with low tolerances.

How can you structure the options to take the client's level of tolerance into account? You can make sure that the menu of choices you offer addresses the client's level of tolerance. If you offer four risky options and one safe one to a client who has a low tolerance, your creativity may have been focused on the wrong end of the scale. Might there have been more than one safe option?

And you can help a client understand whether her or his tolerance for risk is realistic *in this situation*. A client with a high tolerance who wants to make an unrealistic gamble might gain insight if you explain that you think most clients would not bet that steeply against the odds, and *why* most clients wouldn't do that. (But don't claim more than you know. If you don't have much experience with client decision-making, ask a senior lawyer whether most clients would make that bet.) On the other hand, it might be overbearing, if not oppressive, to tell a person with a low tolerance for risk that most clients would make a bet the client does not want to make.

# CHAPTER 10

# COUNSELING CONVERSATIONS WITH TRANSACTIONAL CLIENTS

This chapter explains the ingredients of an extended counseling conversation that would help the client make particularly difficult decisions. Many of these ingredients would also be present in the more abbreviated conversations explained in Chapters 7 and 8.

## §10.1 MOOD, SETTING, AND THE LAWYER'S AFFECT

*Involve the client so you have a genuine conversation.* This is collaborative decision-making. Don't be a talking head. Suppose you're at home, watching television, surfing channels with the remote control in your hand. On the screen you see two or three people sitting in easy chairs in a studio, talking about the great issues of the day. How long will you watch this before moving on to the next channel? They might be discussing a marvelous discovery that will change life as we know it. Why, as soon as you see the talking heads, will you change the channel so quickly that you won't learn this great thing? If you're like most people, you dislike being put in a passive position while somebody talks at you.

In client counseling, a lawyer who's a talking head might explain the choices nonstop for perhaps a half hour and then ask the client whether she has any questions. The client then says her first word: "No." The lawyer concludes by saying, "Well, go home, think about it, and call me when you've decided."

Be an effective active listener, using the techniques explained in §§4.1–4.2.

*Provide helpful respect.* You may know some things the client does not, but the client hired you, can fire you, and therefore is your boss. Moreover, the client has to live with the consequences of this decision long after you've forgotten about it. Why do some lawyers forget this and patronize clients?

> "[I]n almost every advisory relationship, the client is usually untrained in the professional's specialty, while the professional may have seen the client's problem (or variants of it) many times before. There is thus an almost natural tendency to come across to the client as patronizing, pompous, and arrogant. . . . [T]he secret to becoming a good adviser is to [speak] as if you were trying to advise your mother or father . . . with immense amounts of respect. . . ."[1]

***Consider in advance how you will explain legal concepts and terminology.*** Use plain words that accurately describe the concept without implying that you're talking down to the client. Compare two examples. The first flunks this standard:

*1. A lawyer, speaking to a client who owns a gas station and who has just been served with a temporary restraining order:*

> A TRO can be granted while a motion for a preliminary injunction is pending for the purpose of preserving the status quo until the motion can be decided. You've been restrained from selling gasoline from the pumps alleged by the Department of Environmental Protection to be an environmental hazard, and violation of the order is punishable as a contempt. The order is effective until it's vacated, which probably won't be before the court decides the pending motion for a preliminary injunction, which has a return date of next Friday.

*2. Another lawyer, conveying the same information to the same client:*

> A judge can order you not to do something for a short period, which is what has happened here through this document, which lawyers call a temporary restraining order or a TRO. This TRO orders you not to sell gas from the pumps that the Department of Environmental Protection complained to you about last week. If you sell gas from those pumps anyway, the judge can make you pay a fine or even lock you up in jail. The DEP has also asked for another kind of court order called a preliminary injunction, which would do the same thing but for a longer period of time. The judge hasn't given DEP a preliminary injunction, although she might do so later. The TRO—the order that was delivered to you yesterday—will last until the judge decides on Friday whether to issue the other order, the preliminary injunction.

Don't talk to a client as you would to another lawyer. Clients want you to respect their intelligence but to use language that they can understand. This requires careful forethought. Before you sit down with a client, ask yourself what words will most clearly communicate the legal situation to the client.

---

1. David H. Maister, *How to Give Advice*, The American Lawyer, Mar. 1997 57, 57–58.

*Explain the options neutrally.* Remember client-centered lawyering (discussed in Chapter 5). Don't let your wording or body language convey that you like some options better than others. That would put pressure on the client to make a choice she might not make otherwise. If the client wants your recommendation, she will ask for it (see §10.4 for how to answer that question). If the client hasn't asked for your recommendation, keep it to yourself.

*Face the harsh facts.* If the client gets an unrealistically optimistic picture, the decision probably won't be a good one. And clients poorly advised in this way are tempted later to consider ethics complaints and malpractice lawsuits based on a lawyer's failure to warn.

*Create a written list or something else the client can look at during the discussion.* In preparing for this meeting, you'll work out in detail each option's advantages, costs, risks, and chance of success. Your client can better see how these all fit together if you show her something visual. It can be as simple as a handwritten list on a notepad. If the choices and their ramifications are complicated, you might want it typed to get everything on a single page. If the client has to turn from one page to the next, the big picture can disappear.

*If the conversation will be a face-to-face meeting in your office, use an appropriate seating arrangement.* Try not to sit behind a desk, where you look authoritative, distant, and uninterested. (If you were interested, why would you put a big piece of furniture between you and the client?) Sit together at a conference table or in chairs next to each other so you can talk with everything close at hand. The best seating arrangement lets you and the client look together at pieces of paper, such as a list of options or a contract draft.

## §10.2 BEGINNING THE DISCUSSION

If the client is inexperienced in dealing with lawyers, you might explain that this is the client's decision; why it should be the client's decision; how you can help the client make the decision by framing choices and working out their advantages, costs, risks, and chances for success; and how you and the client can work together at doing this. You can dispense with much of these explanations with repeat business clients, who would find them pedantic. But if a client has dealt with lawyers only infrequently, or has dealt in the past with lawyers who have not been very good counselors, the client might really need an orientation.

If any facts or aspects of the law will dominate the decision, you can describe them to the client (or remind the client of them if he already knows). Don't give a detailed recitation unless the client asks for it. (You'e trying to avoid being a talking head.) But if something will be a theme from option to option, it helps to explain it early.

Then, simply outline the options, letting the client see the outline on paper. Describe each one only enough so that the client knows what it is. Then go on to the next option. Don't evaluate the options yet. You're just trying to give the client an overview before you go into the details.

In what sequence should you mention the options? Put yourself in the client's position and ask yourself which sequence would help this client understand the nature of the decision. For example, you might start with the options the client already knows about and work toward the ones that would be news to the client. Or you might start with the most serious options and then mention the more marginal ones.

Then ask the client whether he sees any additional options. Clients can be creative about this. Sometimes they can change some of your ideas into new and additional potential solutions (as the steering committee did in §8.3.2). And sometimes they can think of potential solutions that have escaped you entirely. Clients are closer to the problem than you are, and many of them spend more time than you can thinking about it.

## §10.3 DISCUSSING THE CHOICES AND WHAT THEY WOULD DO

The best transition is to ask the client which options he'd like to talk about first. If the client has no preference, you can discuss them in the same sequence in which you introduced them earlier.

Brainstorming with a client is different from brainstorming with another lawyer. Many clients will assume that their problem-solving skills are inferior to yours, and they'll need your encouragement to believe otherwise. The best encouragement isn't flattery, but instead a sincere interest in how the client thinks and feels about the problem and how it might be resolved. Treat the client as an equal whose views you respect.

## §10.4 IF THE CLIENT ASKS FOR A RECOMMENDATION, SHOULD YOU GIVE ONE?

The lawyer helps, but the client decides. In counseling, that means laying out the choices neutrally, without telling the client which ones you like. If the client isn't interested in an array of options and wants to focus immediately on the one you would recommend, try to persuade the client to choose without your recommendation.

But if the client persists and wants your recommendation at the beginning, then the client is making a choice about how he wants to be counseled, and that choice is one you should respect. But be very careful not to let your own needs—your ego or your tight schedule—delude you about what a client really wants. If it's absolutely clear that this really is what the client feels most comfortable with, you should counsel the client in the manner the client prefers. The client is, after all, the boss. Recommend a solution while explaining its benefits and drawbacks. But mention the alternatives and explain why they're worth considering.

Clients who want to hear only your recommendation might do so for sophisticated reasons. A repeat business client who has dealt with lawyers often and who knows you and trusts your judgment might not want to hear about other options because she's confident that the one you'd recommend is the best. Successful business people know how to use time efficiently and whom to trust. To them, a 30-minute conversation is wasted if a 5-minute conversation would yield the same result.

But three things disappear when you give your recommendation and mention the alternatives only as an afterthought.

One is an opportunity to brainstorm the options with the client. Not only are two minds better than one, but the client usually knows more than you do about some or most of the factual situation as well as the kinds of solutions the client feels more comfortable with. If you suspect that brainstorming might improve the options in a significant way, say something like: "If we can work together for a few minutes to think about the options, it might be a good investment of time. Before I make a recommendation, I want to be sure about the situation."

Another is a process that can give both you and the client assurance that the right decision is being made. People sometimes think of a process as an inconvenient thing one has to endure to get a certain result. But a good process often has its own value even if the same result might be obtained without it. Among other things, a good process creates or deepens confidence that the result is the best one available.

For example, you meet with a client on Monday. At the client's request, you state your recommendation, and the meeting lasts only ten minutes because the client makes a decision on the spot. On Tuesday, you and the client act on that decision, and the action is irrevocable. (No matter how hard you try, you'll never be able to undo it.) On Wednesday and Thursday, lots of unexplored issues keep popping into the client's mind. Finally, on Friday, the client can't stand it any longer and calls you, listing all these issues for you. You explain how, although they're reasonable concerns, none of them would change your recommendation. You have very good reasons, and the client is completely persuaded. After that conversation, the client thinks of a few more unexplored issues. The client might call you again. Or the client might be too embarrassed to do so and might go for a very long time wondering whether your recommendation was really the right thing to do.

Some lawyers would dismiss this client as antsy, but the real problem is that you didn't insist on a process that was thorough enough to give this client confidence from the very beginning that your recommendation was the right thing to do. Some things are too important to be settled just on your recommendation, even if that's how the client wants to handle decision-making at the time.

The third thing that disappears when you give "recommendation only" counseling is full disclosure sufficient to protect yourself from a charge of malpractice if you recommend a solution that fails. Suppose you recommend option A and don't mention option B. Based on what you and the client know at the time, option A is so much better than option B that no reasonable person would seriously consider option B. In other words, you've given exactly the right advice. But later the situation changes. New facts cause option A to fail and to make option B much more attractive. The client hires another lawyer, who sues you in malpractice because you never mentioned option B. You argue that it wouldn't have made any difference because the client would still have chosen option A, which was the better choice when he had to make a decision. But now the client says that if you had explained option B, she would have chosen it. You will spend time in depositions and courtrooms over this.

In addition, "recommendation only" counseling creates a potential for confrontation, which might be either open or hidden. You describe option C and recommend it, telling the client that it is the only thing that will work. The client dislikes option C and says, "I've heard about something else you haven't mentioned. Let's call it option D. There are things about it I like, and I really hope it will work." You've researched this thoroughly and know that the last time option D worked was in 1919, and even then on distinguishable facts. You try to explain why option D won't work. You might persuade the client, and the conversation might end with sincere friendliness on both sides. Or you and the client might argue about it. Or the client doesn't argue, but you see some stiffening body language, after which the client goes away and follows your advice reluctantly, or does nothing, or hires another lawyer. The problem is that you've taken a position, and once you do that, conflict rather than brainstorming can follow. An assertive client might argue with you, and it's difficult to convert arguing into brainstorming. An unassertive client would rather go away than argue, but the problem remains.

All of this is different from the scene in which the client asks you *what you would do if you were in the client's situation*. That is a very good question from a smart client. You should ask the same question of a mechanic who tells you that your eight-year-old car needs a valve job ("If this were your car, what would you do?") or a home contractor who's giving you a quote on an expensive but not urgent repair ("If this were your home, what would you do?").

This client is not really asking for your recommendation. The client wants to know how other informed and responsible people—for example, you—deal with problems like the client's. You can answer while at the same time explaining exactly how your values, goals, tolerance for risk, taste, or situation in life are different from the client's. If you have enough experience to be able to describe how most people in your community decide similar questions, the client might also find that helpful.

## §10.5 ASKING THE CLIENT TO DECIDE

Ask the client to decide among the options. Understandably, the client might want time to think about it. In fact, you ought to encourage that, unless there's some reason for an immediate decision. And don't be surprised if the client telephones with one or two follow-up questions before deciding.

If the decision will be delayed, try to work out a "soft" (flexible) deadline before the client leaves the meeting. Legal work seems to go on interminably because few of the people involved impose deadlines on themselves. A client faced with a tough decision may delay making it and then regret the delay. You can help by asking the client if she wants to set a date by which she will get back to you.

After the client decides, the counseling job is complete, and you and the client then act on that decision.

# CHAPTER 11

# SOME COMMON PROBLEMS IN COUNSELING AND ADVICE

## §11.1 ETHICAL ISSUES IN COUNSELING

*Giving candid and complete advice.* Rule 2.1 of the Model Rules of Professional Conduct requires lawyers to "render candid advice," and in doing so, the "lawyer may refer not only to law but to other considerations such as moral, economic, social, and political factors, that may be relevant to the client's situation." The Comment to Rule 2.1 elaborates:

> A client is entitled to straightforward advice expressing the lawyer's honest assessment. Legal advice often involves unpleasant facts and alternatives that a client may be disinclined to confront. In presenting advice, a lawyer endeavors to sustain the client's morale and may put advice in as acceptable a form as honesty permits. However, a lawyer should not be deterred from giving candid advice by the prospect that the advice will be unpalatable to the client.
>
> Advice couched in narrow legal terms may be of little value to a client, especially when practical considerations, such as cost or effects on other people, are predominant.... It is proper for a lawyer to refer to relevant moral and ethical considerations in giving advice. Although a lawyer is not a moral advisor as such, moral and ethical considerations impinge upon most legal questions and may decisively influence how the law will be applied.

Rule 1.4 requires you to "explain a matter to the extent reasonably necessary to permit the client to make informed decisions." The Comment to Rule 1.4 notes that, in many instances, the client can make an informed decision only if you explain the damage that some of the options under consideration might cause to others:

> The client should have sufficient information to participate intelligently in decisions concerning the objectives of the representation and the means by which they are to be pursued, to the extent the client is willing and able to do so. . . . The guiding principle is that the lawyer should fulfill reasonable client expectations for information consistent with the duty to act in the client's best interests, and the client's overall requirements as to the character of representation.

***When the client decides to do something illegal.*** Illegality can happen on more than one level. One client might want to commit a crime. Another client might decide to do something that involves an increased risk of negligence or contract breach liability. Ethics law treats these possibilities differently.

Under Rule 1.2(d) of the Model Rules:

> A lawyer shall not counsel a client to engage, or assist a client, in conduct that the lawyer knows is criminal or fraudulent, but a lawyer may discuss the legal consequences of any proposed course of conduct with a client and may counsel or assist a client to make a good faith effort to determine the validity, scope, meaning or application of the law.

You may not suggest an option that involves committing a crime or fraud. Suppose your client makes a false statement to the other party. The other party's lawyer asks that in the written contract your client make a representation identical to that statement. If your client knew when she made the statement that it was false, she probably made an intentional misrepresentation, also known as a fraudulent misrepresent or fraud. If you know it's a misrepresentation but draft it into the contract anyway, you may have participated in the fraud, which Rule 1.2(d) prohibits.

But if a client asks you whether a particular act would be illegal, you may answer the question, regardless of what the answer might be. If you say that the act would be illegal and if the client then asks what would happen if the client were to do it anyway, you may answer that question as well. Depending on the act at issue, you might say that the client could be made to pay damages in tort or contract, or you might explain the judge's sentencing discretion if the act is a crime. If the client further asks you to predict whether the client would be held liable or prosecuted or convicted, you may answer that, too. For example, if the client has a store and wants to open it for business on Sundays, and if your state or county has a Sunday-closing law that has not been enforced in generations, you may tell the client that opening on Sundays is technically illegal, but that there is virtually no chance of the client's being prosecuted. Why may you do that? If law—as practicing lawyers know it—is "[w]hat officials do about disputes,"[1] you're explaining the law to your client.[2]

***When the client makes a decision that you consider immoral.*** Ethics law gives you a choice between two alternatives. You may act on the client's wishes. Or you may withdraw (stop doing work for the client).[3] Your withdrawal probably

---

1. Karl N. Llewellyn, *The Bramble Bush* 3 (1930).
2. Monroe H. Freedman, *Lawyers' Ethics in an Adversary System* 59–60 (1975).
3. Model Rule 1.16(b)(4).

would not cause the client to change the decision. Another lawyer can probably be found who won't object as you did.

Usually, it's more effective to appeal to the client's self-interest. You might develop a creative plan that does something for the client's interests while reducing or eliminating the moral problem and without identifying it as a moral problem.

For example, suppose the client is a real estate developer who has quietly bought up a city block made up of apartment houses. The tenants are all low-income, and the client wants to tear down the buildings and construct a large corporate office complex with upscale stores on the street level. The client has already emptied most of the apartments by refusing to renew leases as they expire and by offering a few thousand dollars each to tenants who would move out while their leases are still in effect. He predicts that, if this continues, nearly all the apartments will be empty within a few months. But about a dozen tenants have declared that they refuse to move, and each of them has a lease that extends long past the scheduled date of demolition. The client calls these people "the resisters."

He intends to demolish, on a 24-hour-a-day schedule, the buildings in which the resisters do not live, which is legal in that part of town even though the resisters wouldn't be able to get much sleep. The client won't make access to the resisters' apartments easy during demolition, and he will cut off the resisters' utilities from time to time, using "demolition safety" as an excuse. You told him that it would be illegal to cut off utilities unless it was really required for safety reasons, and he asked whether the resisters could easily prove that the cutoffs were unnecessary. When you answered that proof would be hard, although not impossible, he chuckled.

What can you do to persuade this client that it would be in his own self-interest to treat these people better? Sometimes a client may be influenced by predictions of bad things that could happen to the client. But the facts here won't support that. This client can probably get away with it if he's cunning enough. You're not willing to withdraw, and even if you were, it would make no difference because the client can replace you with another lawyer who's not bothered by such things.

The key is to find an incentive that makes sense within the client's way of thinking. Can you show the client that more civilized methods of persuading the resisters to leave would cost less? Can you think up an act of generosity on the client's part that would solve the resisters' housing problems while producing a benefit for the client that he considers worthwhile? Some clients instinctively think narrowly while ignoring the effects of good and bad publicity. And the tax code can at times be helpful. Money spent in some ways is not taxed or is taxed less than money spent in other ways. You can't know the true cost of any transaction until its tax consequences are factored in.

## §11.2 WHEN THE LAWYER SUSPECTS THAT THE CLIENT'S STATED GOAL MIGHT NOT REALLY BE WHAT THE CLIENT WANTS

Sometimes a client needs a detached observer, such as a lawyer, to sense an inner truth about the client's situation and then help the client face it. That is particularly so when a client assumes or has been forced into thinking that a particular legal solution is what they should be seeking. How can you help here? Listen with your heart rather than with the rational part of your brain. Then ask questions that probe the client's feelings. When you read the following article, notice how the lawyer listened and how the lawyer asked questions.

### STEVEN KEEVA, WHAT CLIENTS WANT
#### ABA Journal, June 2002, at 49

"If you can discover what your clients really want . . . then, as a lawyer, you are really empowered," [lawyer Arnie] Herz says. "We're trained to size up a situation—the client has X problem or Y problem. We pin things down, then move through the process with blinders on. But life's not like that . . . ."

[When] Macie Scherick . . . hired Herz . . . all she needed was for him to draft documents so she could sell her 50 percent share of a SoHo art gallery. At least, that's all she *said* she needed. . . .

But Herz sensed there might be more to think about. He asked Scherick about the business and about her partner of 15 years, and he listened carefully to her answers.

The result? . . . Scherick [recalls that Hertz] "profoundly transformed my life." . . .

Herz says [that clients] "are apt to accept legal solutions that don't serve them as well as they might."

That's exactly what Scherick was ready to do. But as she talked about selling her stake in the gallery, Herz didn't hear a woman who wanted out. He heard a woman who loved her work but had been intimidated by her business partner. At the time, Scherick had a 2-year-old child, plus another one on the way. Her partner was insisting that the demands of motherhood were inhibiting the gallery's success and, therefore her own. Scherick said she was willing to step aside.

But Herz heard between the lines. "For Macie, what first appeared to be a simple legal transaction powered by a solid business rationale turned out to be a complex situation involving two disempowered people," says Herz. "She . . . was fearful of confrontation, intimidated by her partner's emotions and aggressiveness, and not aware of her legal rights. So she was brought to the brink of selling a business she loved, was good at, and that was rightfully hers."

When Herz explained to Scherick that she was legally entitled to stay in the business, and that her partner could not force dissolution or push her out, she didn't believe it. "But then she began to see that she was not powerless," says Herz. "In fact, it became clear to her that, with all the legal leverage she had, she held the power and not her partner. . . . You have to identify and acknowledge any fear and/or anger or confusion that clients may be experiencing. When you do that, the relationship is totally transformed. They then know what it means to be heard, because you're seeing their true interests. . . ."

[Herz says he asks his clients to] "step outside the legal situation [and] think about what they'd like their lives to look like three or four months down the line. Suddenly they see possibilities that never would have occurred to them before."

Once the shift occurred in her understanding of what brought her to Herz in the first place, Scherick allowed him to negotiate a fair deal for her. The result was that the partner left the business to start her own.

Scherick, along with a new partner, continues to run the business, which has grown substantially in both revenues and square footage. Their Sears Peyton Gallery is about to double its space in a move to Chelsea, the very epicenter of the New York art world.

## §11.3 WHEN THE CLIENT MAKES A DECISION THE LAWYER CONSIDERS EXTREMELY UNWISE

Looking at the client's interests alone, a decision is extremely unwise if it would cause a great deal more difficulty for the client than it would solve, or if it would do a much less effective job of solving the client's problems than options the client rejects.

This isn't the same as a decision that you wouldn't make if you were in the client's position. The client, not the lawyer, has to live with the consequences of the decision. If the decision reflects the client's tastes and values rather than yours, there's nothing troubling about that.

Why might a client choose an option that would cause many more problems than it would solve—or that would do a much less effective job of solving the client's problems than other options would? The client might be ineffectual at making decisions in general. Or the client might be either much less willing or much more willing to take risks than you expected. Or the client might disagree with your predictions of what the various options will cause.

Among the things clients hire lawyers for is to warn them of trouble, and the client who makes an extremely unwise decision is entitled to warning. That client is also entitled to ignore your warning after hearing it. The client is the one who will live with the consequences of the decision. The client decides whether to make risky bets or safer ones. And sometimes clients turn out to be right when they reject their lawyers' predictions.

How can you deliver this warning? Don't give a lecture. Instead, raise the matter through questions and through statements of concern about the client's needs. The questions should probe so you can find out why the client is making this decision. You're looking for the places where the client's thinking diverges radically from your own.

A good way to express your concern is to say that you're worried about the client or about some aspect of the situation. Make it clear that you'll act faithfully on whatever decision the client makes, but because of the matter's importance, you want to make sure that the client understands the risks and consequences.

## §11.4 WHEN THE CLIENT HAS BEEN PERSUADED BY COGNITIVE ILLUSIONS

A *cognitive illusion* or *cognitive bias* is a pattern of thought that causes a person to reason unrealistically, especially about predictions. Here's an example:

> In researching what classes he wanted to take for his third year, [Frank] had examined the course catalogue and looked up the student evaluation results for all the classes and professors in which he was interested. Having done an exhaustive review of all the possibilities, Frank completed his registration form and got on line at the Registrar's office to turn it in. While on line, he got into a conversation with a student from his first-year section, not his friend or someone he knew well, but an acquaintance. They compared their registration lists to see what they were going to take, and the other

student commented that he had heard that a professor teaching a course Frank was signing up for was a real bore and that the course sounded a lot better than it really was. This surprised Frank, because he had looked up the course evaluations, and the students in the classes the previous few years had given the professor above average reviews. Nevertheless, Frank . . . changed his registration form right there on line to substitute a different course.

[Frank was later asked why he did this.] . . . did he have any particular reason to trust the other student's opinion (no, he did not really know the student very well); did he change his mind because the opinion expressed related to something that would not be captured on an evaluation, such as whether the teacher was a tough grader (no, it was based purely on the "boring" comment, which was one of the subjects covered in the evaluations); had the spontaneous hearsay opinion confirmed anything else he'd heard about the professor (no, in fact all he knew about the professor was the generally positive commentary from the published evaluations). Having done exhaustive research into course evaluations, Frank had accumulated dozens, if not hundreds, of student evaluations of the professor that convinced him that the course was worth taking. But all that research got pushed aside on the hearsay opinion offered by a student that Frank did not even know very well.[4]

Frank might have acted on any of several cognitive illusions, and without asking him further questions, it's hard to say which persuaded him.

One might have been a false assumption that anecdotal evidence trumps empirical evidence. The anecdotal evidence here amounted to rumor from a student Frank didn't know to be reliable. The empirical evidence that Frank had studied (the student evaluations) was impressive. But people often do what Frank did because empirical evidence seems cold and distant while anecdotal evidence is more immediate and vivid (though often unreliable).

Another cognitive illusion is a false assumption that the last information we receive—or the first we receive—is more valid than other information. People are often persuaded by *when* they get information, although its quality has no relationship to when it is delivered, which may be merely coincidental. Other cognitive illusions are explained in the next section of this chapter.

Many clients are tempted by cognitive illusions when making decisions. Trying to argue a client out of a cognitive illusion usually doesn't work and can make a client resentful. What can you do? The most effective thing is to ask questions—like the questions Frank was asked—and to ask them respectfully and with genuine curiosity (not like a classroom Socratic dialog). It's easier for the client to abandon the illusion if you *help* the client see the problem than if you try to force the client to see it.

What if the client won't give up the illusion? That's the client's prerogative. You've fulfilled your obligation if you make it possible for the client to see that it is an illusion.

---

4. Joseph W. Rand, *Understanding Why Good Lawyers Go Bad: Using Case Studies in Teaching Cognitive Bias in Legal Decision-Making*, 9 Clinical L. Rev. 731, 751–752 (2003). See also Ian Weinstein, *Don't Believe Everything You Think: Cognitive Bias in Legal Decision-Making*, 9 Clinical L. Rev. 793 (2003).

## §11.5 GUARDING AGAINST YOUR OWN COGNITIVE ILLUSIONS

What causes doctors to make mistakes? Much research has been done to answer that question, and the studies appear to show that a large proportion of the diagnostic errors made by doctors are caused by cognitive illusions.[5] Although the legal profession has not been studied in the same way, it seems likely that cognitive illusions cause a substantial proportion of lawyers' mistakes.

"Most physicians are not aware of their cognitive mistakes."[6] Probably, most lawyers aren't either. While you're interpreting facts and evidence and making predictions about what will happen, examine your own thinking to make sure that you are not being influenced by any of the following:

*Availability bias* is "the tendency to judge the likelihood of an event by the ease with which relevant examples come to mind."[7] This is why Frank (in §11.4) rejected his own empirical evidence after someone told him an anecdote. Although the example below is from criminal defense work, it makes the point vividly.

Suppose that last month Judge Patel sentenced one of your clients to the maximum penalty available for the crime of which the client was convicted. You'll appear before Judge Patel again tomorrow with Lusardi, another client who has been charged with the same type of crime. Lusardi asks you to predict what will happen if he pleads guilty. Will Judge Patel again impose the maximum sentence, or something close to it? You're tempted to predict exactly that because you saw her do it only last month. And many lawyers would be tempted to make the same prediction.

But what do you really know? Suppose that in the past 12 months Judge Patel has sentenced 100 defendants for this type of crime. Of that data, you know only 1%—your client from last month. It's possible that Judge Patel sentenced all the other 99 defendants to the maximum, which would give her a 100% maximum-sentence rate for this crime. It's also possible that your client from last month was the only one sentenced to the maximum, and that Judge Patel was remarkably lenient in each of the other 99 cases. If that's true, she hands down the maximum sentence only 1% of the time—not 100%.

You don't know any of this. All you know is what you saw last month. You'd be tempted to say to Lusardi, "You're looking at something like the maximum sentence, which is what she did to one of my clients last month." But if you say that, you will have been seduced by availability bias. An example was available—an anecdote, really—and it biased you so you didn't investigate further. You assumed that the anecdote was representative of everything.

To avoid availability bias, refuse to be seduced by an example and instead investigate the whole picture. Here, you would find out what Judge Patel did in *many* of the cases where a defendant was convicted of this crime. You might not be able to find out what she did in all of them. But you can learn enough to estimate what the pattern is. For example, ask lawyers who are in her courtroom regularly.

---

5. Jerome Groopman, *How Doctors Think* (2007).
6. *Id.* at 277.
7. *Id.* at 64.

*Confirmation bias* causes people to focus on information that confirms their preconceptions while ignoring information that challenges their preconceptions. Examples are all around us in everyday life—typically when you see someone itemizing facts, evidence, and ideas to justify what they like.

*Search satisficing* or *satisfaction of search* is the tendency to stop searching for explanations once you've found *one* you find convincing. The explanation you found might not be the right explanation or the best one. It's just the first one you found. If you call off the search because you've found an explanation, you won't know about other explanations because your mind closed as soon as you found one. You assumed there were no others. The one you found might not be the best one. Some of the others may be much better.

*Confidence illusions* frequently infect professionals who are conscious of their own expertise. All around us, experts confidently predict the future and turn out to be wrong. Predictions by experts in the stock market, for example, are wrong more often than they're right. On cable news channels, commentators confidently make predictions that are interesting at the time but later turn out to be flat-out wrong. The experts making these predictions are often victims of confidence illusions. Even nonexperts overestimate their own abilities. Most drivers believe they have above-average driving skills, which is mathematically impossible.[8]

Expertise can actually cause errors by inducing confidence illusions. If you're an expert lawyer, you may overestimate your tendency to be right.

---

8. Tom Vanderbilt, *Traffic: Why We Drive the Way We Do (and What It Says About Us)* (2009).

# PART IV

# TRANSACTIONAL NEGOTIATION

# CHAPTER 12

# NEGOTIATION BY LAWYERS IN TRANSACTIONS

## §12.1 THE TWO NEGOTIATIONS—BUSINESS ISSUES AND LEGAL ISSUES

Section 1.4 explains the difference between business issues and legal issues.

In most deals, the business issues—price, what the price buys, quantity, delivery schedule, and so on—are negotiated by the parties directly. The lawyers typically aren't part of that negotiation and often don't know that it's happening. After the parties have settled the business terms, they send the deal to their lawyers to "draw up the contract." Business people often think that what the lawyers will do is pure draftsmanship. But it's much more than that. The lawyers don't just "draw up the contract." They conduct a lawyers' negotiation in which they resolve the legal issues, which are explained in the next section of this chapter. The written contract is the result of that negotiation, which is centered on "translating the business deal into contract concepts."[1]

Litigators sometimes assume that deal lawyers are involved in the money—that deal lawyers have something to say about the price or the delivery schedule or what's being bought. Usually that's not true. If a deal lawyer were to meddle in these matters on a daily business, as though she had some expertise in what's a good delivery schedule, clients would become justifiably upset. Negotiating the business issues is usually outside a lawyer's zone of expertise.

Litigators can be surprised by this because in dispute negotiation, if there's money, the lawyers are in charge of it. Although every client makes the ultimate decision about whether to agree to a settlement, the tort plaintiff-client, for example, doesn't negotiate in advance what the money is and then ask the lawyer to

---

1. Tina L. Stark, *Drafting Contracts: How and Why Lawyers Do What They Do* 6 (2007).

resolve the legal issues involved. The money *is* a legal issue because the law—not the market—can decide how much the plaintiff gets.

To a dispute negotiator, what a deal lawyer does can seem trivial. If the business people have settled everything, what's the deal lawyer for? Actually the business people have *not* settled everything, and the *prospective* legal issues—the ones that look forward to the future—are far more complicated in a deal than in litigation. In a tort settlement, for example, the legal issues concerning the future are the procedure for dismissing the lawsuit and the practicalities of making sure the plaintiff gets paid—both of which are routine and involve little or no professional creativity.

But in a deal, nearly all the legal issues are about the future. Even the ones that seem to be about the past or the present are really about the future. If the lawyers agree to have the seller of a factory represent and warrant that the factory has never been used to manufacture items that contain environmentally hazardous materials (the past) and that no environmentally hazardous materials are on the property or in the ground under the property (the present), it isn't because the buyer enjoys knowing history or present conditions. It's to provide the buyer with remedies if environmentally hazardous materials are found on site *in the future*.

Every deal is a mixture of opportunity and risk. And nearly everything that deal lawyers do in their negotiation is to preserve and sometimes enlarge each party's opportunities for future gain, while limiting and allocating the parties' future risks.

In a lawsuit, the negotiation usually *ends* the parties' connection to each other. What matters is what the parties *have already done*—the tort itself, for example. But in a deal, the two negotiations *begin* the connection, at least for this deal. (They might have done previous deals with each other.) What matters is what the parties *will do*—whether and how they'll perform on their promises and what will happen if they don't.

Negotiating for that future is a tough professional challenge. It's what deal lawyers do.

While haggling over legal terms, the lawyers are producing a written contract. Clients sometimes think there's too much haggling and the lawyers are taking too long and costing too much money, just to draft a document that seems incomprehensible. Clients can feel this way because the legal issues are outside their zone of expertise, just as the business issues are outside the lawyers' zone of expertise. "Clients often complain that lawyers don't understand business and the sorts of risks that business people take every day. . . . On the other hand, lawyers often complain that their clients don't understand the extent of a legal risk."[2]

The distinction between the two negotiations can become blurred. Sometimes, for example, a lawyer realizes that a business issue was not resolved in the parties' negotiation, and the client, for convenience, asks the lawyer to resolve it in the lawyers' negotiation. Sometimes a client with little experience or business skills asks a lawyer specializing in the type of transaction to do both negotiations, which will merge into a single negotiation. And very often there is no legal-issues

---

2. Robert H. Mnookin, Scott R. Peppet & Andrew S. Tulumello, *Beyond Winning: Negotiating to Create Value in Deals and Disputes* 149 (2000).

negotiation because those issues were decided unilaterally long ago by a lawyer who drafted the standard-form contract offered by a business to a consumer.

But the bigger the transaction, the more likely there will be two negotiations with lawyers on both sides to settle the legal issues. Think of that as a lawyer-to-lawyer negotiated contract.

## §12.2 WHAT TO NEGOTIATE—THE LEGAL ISSUES

Much of the lawyers' negotiation concerns risk. Each lawyer imagines the ways in which her client could suffer in this deal. Then the two lawyers haggle about allocating risks between the parties. Imagine the lawyers sitting across from each other at a table, each lawyer pushing her client's risks to the other lawyer's side of the table and the other lawyer trying to push them back again.

It isn't exactly like that. First, the lawyers typically won't negotiate across from each other at a table (see §15.1 for why). Second, if the lawyers are problem-solving, each will be willing to accept some risks but will expect the other party to accept some risks as well (see Chapter 14). And risk isn't the only thing to negotiate. Each lawyer looks for ways to preserve and perhaps enlarge her client's opportunities as well. Opportunities can vary greatly from one type of deal to another, and it's hard to generalize about them. But risks can recur from deal to deal.

***Standards.*** Whenever something could vary, a standard is needed as a benchmark.[3] How much is good enough? Numerical standards, such as the purchase price, are simple and clear. A payment that's a penny short isn't good enough. A penny more than the contract number is nice but unnecessary.

If a party has agreed to do something that isn't quantifiable, there's a chance the standard can't be exact. A promise by that party to *try* to accomplish something usually isn't good enough for the other party. *Trying* could be minimal and half-hearted. "Reasonable efforts" requires more. "Commercially reasonable efforts" can be more clear because it refers to what people in the relevant industry or market consider reasonable. "Best efforts" is a higher standard than efforts that are "reasonable."

The highest standard is succeeding rather than just trying. Often that's exactly what the other party has bargained for. A buyer doesn't want a seller to make best efforts to deliver the goods on time. He wants them on time, and anything less should be breach. A standard lower than success creates risks for that buyer.

But where a party promises a service for which success depends on factors outside that party's control, the party should avoid promising success. In a contract between a political candidate and a campaign consultant, for example, the consultant would be foolish to promise that his advice will cause the candidate to win an election. Too many other factors will determine the winner, and a standard of success would put the consultant at enormous risk of breach.

---

3. Stark, *supra* note 1, at 309–310.

*The "supposed to"s—covenants and conditions.* In the business negotiation, the parties will have agreed that each of them is "supposed to" do certain things. For each "supposed to," the lawyers have to make a choice. Is it a covenant or a condition or both? Often the answer is obvious. Sometimes it's not, and then it can become a negotiation issue between the lawyers. Each lawyer will worry about what happens if the party doesn't do what she's "supposed to" do. When the lawyers negotiate whether it's a covenant, a condition, or both, they're deciding the consequences of its not being done. They'll allocate between the parties the *risk* of its not being done. Section 6.7 and Appendices C and D explain why and how.

*Reliance on facts and factual assumptions:* Every party enters a deal relying on certain facts. A risk is the possibility that they might not be true. If the client assumes a fact—rather than knowing it firsthand—the client needs protection in the contract. The most common methods of providing that protection are due diligence, representations, warranties, and promises by the other party to facilitate the client's due diligence. Section 6.7 and Appendix E explain why and how.

If only the other party can know whether those facts really are true, do three things.

First, ask for substantiation ("Would you provide audited copies of those financial records?"). Second, negotiate for opportunities for your client to do due diligence (see Appendix E). Third, ask the other party to represent and warrant in the written agreement that the facts on which your client relies are true (see Appendix E). If the other party misrepresents facts or breaches a warranty, that creates grounds for some of the remedies discussed in Appendix E.

If the other party refuses to represent and warrant a fact that ought to be within the other party's knowledge, that's a danger sign. It's natural for lawyers to haggle over how broad or narrow a representation and warranty will be. But a flat out refusal to make any kind of representation or warranty suggests that the fact your client is assuming might not be true. If that fact is truly important to the deal, you may need to warn your client of what's happening in the negotiation.

These risks run both ways. Your client's risk can be reduced through representations and warranties you obtain from the other party. But at the same time, your client's risk can be enlarged by representations and warranties the other side obtains from you. The broader *those* representations and warranties are, the greater is the risk that liability for your client could be created inadvertently through faulty memory or miscommunication among your client's employees or between your client and you. By accident your client might represent and warrant something that is not true.

*Exit or endgame.*[4] Who should be able to terminate the contract and under what conditions? If one party can terminate at will, and the other can terminate only when certain conditions are satisfied, the party whose termination power is limited by conditions is the one at greater risk. If the deal turns out to be bad one, one party can leave it (terminate) more easily than the other. Here and in many other ways, conditions can be used as a risk allocation device. Appendices C and D explain how.

---

4. *Id.* at 157–163.

In addition, what are the consequences of termination? What will each party get to keep? Will the terminating party have to pay something to the other party? Your cell phone contract probably requires you to pay a fee if you terminate early. And if you terminate an apartment lease, you might not get your security deposit back. In both instances, you signed a standard-form contract into which lawyers for the cell phone company and the landlord have drafted provisions protecting their clients against the risk of early termination by you. (Actually, the landlord might have asked you to sign a standard-form lease sold by a legal forms company and drafted by a lawyer the landlord never met. Because landlords buy the forms, that lawyer will have drafted to protect all landlords, not just yours.)

*The general provisions.* These appear near the end of the contract. Among other things, the lawyers should negotiate which state's or country's law will govern the contract (a choice-of-law clause); how and where disputes will be decided (a forum selection or arbitration clause); the extent to which a party can assign its rights or delegate its duties to a nonparty (called an anti-assignment clause, although it also covers delegations and could limit rather than prohibit); and what events outside the parties' control will excuse nonperformance of duties (a force majeure clause).

## §12.3 MUCH OF LEGAL-ISSUE NEGOTIATION IS REALLY ABOUT LABELS

Because law treats things according to the way they're labeled, a lawyer tries to negotiate into the contract the labels that best advance the client's interests—as long as they're labels the law will accept. Here's an example:

A young man and a young woman begin a romance. Each has $15,000. They decide to begin a business with those funds, and the young man turns over his money to the young woman for that purpose.

Did they intend to form a joint venture? A partnership? Has the young woman been appointed an agent? A bailee? A trustee? Did the young man make a gift? A loan? Are they pooling their resources, each thinking about the possibility of marriage? The couple didn't talk about any of this. And, except for the possibility of marriage, they may not even have thought about it. They just did what they did.

They mention the $15,000 to a lawyer. The lawyer points out that because their business relationship is not yet labeled, their individual rights to share in the profits and their individual liability for losses, torts, and taxes have not been settled. The lawyer adds some possibilities that are consistent with but not yet suggested by the facts, such as forming a corporation. They ask which label is best for them. The answer is complicated because of the advantages and disadvantages of each label. The lawyer explains them, and the couple choose a label. (This is counseling, as explained in Chapters 7–11.)

The lawyer then lists the things that have to be done for the law to accept the label they've chosen. For example, if they decide that the money is a loan, the lawyer will draw up a loan agreement clarifying that and setting out the terms of the loan. Or if they would prefer that pooling the money be considered an act of partnership formation, the lawyer will draw up a partnership agreement. Or if they decide to incorporate, the lawyer will draw up the papers necessary to form a corporation.

If the young man hires one lawyer and the young woman hires another, the lawyers will negotiate the labels.

Often lawyers work out the labels without asking clients to make decisions. Suppose one company is buying a factory from another, and the deal has been turned over to lawyers for their negotiation. In a conversation before lawyers became involved, the selling company told the buying company that environmentally hazardous materials have never been used in the factory. The buyer's lawyer cares about this because if hazardous materials have seeped into the ground, whoever owns the property when they are discovered has the initial liability for removing them, which can be extraordinarily expensive.

Is the seller's statement a representation or a warranty? Appendix E explains how the burdens of proof are different, and the remedies are also different. This doesn't have to be an either/or situation. The statement can be both a representation *and* a warranty. The buyer's lawyer wants it to be both so that if something goes wrong, the buyer would have flexibility about what remedy to seek and what to try to prove.

The time to settle this is now—at the deal stage—and not later if fighting breaks out. It's much cheaper and easier to do it now rather than pay litigators to get a court to decide. The buyer's lawyer calls the seller's lawyer and says, "Your client has assured mine that no hazmats are on site. Naturally, we'll need a rep and warranty to that effect." After some haggling, wording is inserted into the contract that labels the statement both a representation and a warranty. The haggling is about the labels.

## §12.4 PREPARING TO NEGOTIATE

Preparation is perhaps 80% or 90% of the work done by an effective lawyer in negotiation. The overwhelming majority of negotiation time is not spent in discussions with the other side. It's spent *preparing* for those discussions.

Figure out what you want—exactly, not vaguely. What precisely are your goals and agenda? What strategies will you use to accomplish your goals?

How does the deal look to the other party and the other lawyer? You can't persuade people unless you understand them.

How will the other party make money? What's important to the other party, not just in this deal but generally in the other party's industry and market? What might the other party be worried about?

What is the other lawyer like? Again, you can't persuade a person without understanding her. What's the other lawyer's style of practicing law? What strategies might she use? What comments by you might resonate well, or badly, with her?

## §12.5 WORKING WITH THE CLIENT DURING THE NEGOTIATION

For reasons explained in Chapter 5, the client has the ultimate say in nearly everything you do. Some clients want active involvement. Others want to be consulted only as necessary.

If a legal issue turns out to be something about which the client would have preferences, ask the client how she wants the issue handled. You can do that before negotiating the issue. Or you can negotiate agreement on it and on condition that it's tentative subject to client approval. Some legal issues require enough client involvement that you'll need to provide advice or counseling (Chapters 7–11).

Never add to or change the business deal without first obtaining client approval. Never negotiate business issues at all unless specifically authorized by your client. If you're not sure whether something is a business issue, ask your client. Lawyers don't understand business issues as well as business clients do. And the business deal negotiated by the parties may have a delicate balance. If you change anything without client approval, you might alter that balance, with consequences you might not foresee. A change can also require business actions that are impractical in ways your client understands, but you might not.

At the end, you'll have a final-draft contract for your client to sign. Unless the client has done this kind of deal many times before, explain the contract to the client. If the client really wants to know the details, explain them. If the client just wants to know the most important parts, explain them. Do all this before asking the client to sign. Unless this deal is utterly routine for this client, she can rightly feel marginalized when a lawyer simply hands her a document and says, "Sign here."

# CHAPTER 13

# INTERESTS, RIGHTS, AND POWER

Every transaction occurs against a backdrop of the parties' relative interests, rights, and power.

## §13.1 EACH PARTY'S INTERESTS

Every deal is a mixture of opportunity and risk. A party's main interest is to enlarge opportunities while reducing risk. But the details of opportunity and risk differ greatly from one deal to another.

During the business issue negotiation, the parties focus mostly on the opportunities. The risks they worry about are primarily business risks. For example, a seller committing itself to sell over the next year for a price the parties fix today probably is worried about whether the seller's own costs might rise during that time. If the seller's costs rise above the contract price, the seller will lose money on the deal. A lawyer can help by suggesting an escalator clause, but the seller probably already thought of that. It's an obvious device to a business person.

Instead, the lawyer will focus on risks where law has a role. Mnookin, Peppet, and Tulumello explain:

> Transactional lawyers are experts at thinking about what might possibly go wrong with a deal and how to protect their clients from avoidable risks and unwise commitments. The hard question is what level of risk a client should accept—which risks are important and which less so. . . .
>
> Lawyers are involved in . . . complex leases, real estate sales, loan agreements, mergers and acquisitions, corporate financing, compensation contracts, partnership

agreements, and licensing of intellectual property and patents. Each context has its special risks and opportunities.

[A]ttorneys come to understand these risks through past experience—working a particular kind of deal repeatedly, perhaps initially with more senior colleagues who can identify typical problems. . . .[1]

## §13.2 EACH PARTY'S RIGHTS

*Rights* are principles that demonstrate the legitimacy or fairness of a party's position. They can be based on formal legal rules from statutes, case law, and administrative regulations. In transactional negotiations, they can also be grounded on general expectations of behavior, such as industry standards or common practice in a market. The parties' rights provide context in transactional bargaining.

Deal lawyers leverage their clients' rights by making arguments. An *argument* is a group of ideas, arranged logically to convince somebody to do something or agree to something. Although all legal arguments have some similarities, argument in negotiation is unique. You're not trying to convince a neutral decision maker; instead, you are trying to persuade someone whose interests aren't the same as your client's.

***Develop a detailed and organized argument.*** Effective legal argument must be both well developed and well organized. Detailed argumentation requires a crisp, explicit statement of the rule or standard you're invoking, a specific description of the relevant facts, and a conclusion.

***Engage in multi-dimensional reasoning.*** The strength of your argument can be increased if you expand the number of rules or standards on which you rely or the facts or both.

Suppose you represent a manufacturer that wants to build a small factory near a residential community. In negotiation with a community group, you can argue simply that the local zoning ordinance allows for the siting of the factory on this property. Alternatively, you can make an argument like this:

> As I'm sure city officials have told you, the zoning ordinances allow us to build the factory here without the issuance of a permit or variance. Additionally, three similar factories have been built in other areas zoned I-A in the past five years without any city intervention. But most importantly, consider the jobs this factory will create for your community. Each of the other two factories we operate employs 50 people from the surrounding community. Finally, as to your fears about air pollution, our consultant's report shows, our environmental safety record is excellent.

While the first argument addresses solely the narrow issue of the zoning ordinance, the second argument raises not only that issue, but also policy reasons (the city's precedent with such projects) and factual support (increased employment and environmental safety).

---

1. Robert H. Mnookin, Scott R. Peppet & Andrew S. Tulumello, *Beyond Winning: Negotiating to Create Value in Deals and Disputes* 252, 254 (2000).

*Design a balanced argument.* Balance can create an appearance of reasonableness. In negotiation, that's particularly important because the other party starts out with interests inconsistent with yours and thus treats you warily. By demonstrating that you understand the strengths and weaknesses on both sides of the issue, you show that your assessment of rights is solid and that your reasoning is sound. The legitimacy of your argument will be affected significantly by your acknowledgment of any weaknesses on your side.

## §13.3 EACH PARTY'S POWER

Power is "the ability to coerce someone to do something he would not otherwise do."[2] Although rights can coerce the party against whom they are enforced, power is coercion without resorting to enforcement of legal rights.

For some people and in some negotiations, relative power is the determinative factor. For example, when you want to buy a computer, the basic terms of the contract—the price, available accessories and software, and warranty—aren't negotiable. When you find the computer you want to buy, you must accept the terms on which the manufacturer will let it be sold. But when General Motors wants to buy a computer, it can either dictate terms to a much smaller company or negotiate on an equal footing with a company large enough to have market power that matches GM's.

Even in a setting where one party starts out with a substantial power disadvantage, relative power doesn't necessarily determine the result. For example, car dealers have bargaining resources vastly superior to those of most car buyers. But dealers must sell in a competitive market. During certain times of the year, dealers need to sell cars to get them out of inventory. At those times, buyers may have significant power, at least with regard to the valuing of the trade-in, the financing package, or the availability of some options. Thus, relative power can be variable and doesn't always determine the negotiation's outcome.

*Economic power.* A party's resources obviously can influence a negotiation. When a large corporation negotiates to acquire a smaller, family-run business, for example, the acquiring company will probably have at its disposal a much greater staff of lawyers, accountants, and tax experts.

But parties with large resources may suffer from limitations on their power, and parties with ostensibly fewer resources may have access to other means of economic power. A large corporation buying a smaller company may be involved in many other transactions and some litigation and may be able to devote only limited legal staff to this deal. And the privately owned company may have retained a small, boutique law firm that specializes in representing "underdogs" in such negotiations. And in labor-management negotiations, the employees may have an advantage if they are few in number, have highly specialized skills, and operate expensive and complicated machinery. The company

---

2. William L. Ury et al., *Getting Disputes Resolved: Designing Systems to Cut the Costs of Conflict* 7 (1988).

may have invested heavily in equipment, and it may be cheaper to raise pay than to let that equipment sit idle while hard-to-replace workers are on strike.

*Expertise.* In some negotiations one party has greater expertise on certain issues involved in the transaction, and that knowledge can result in a power imbalance. Moreover, the more information that a party has about a particular situation, the more likely that she will understand its context and will be able to make a quick decision even with limited resources. Imagine, for instance, a company official with no computer background who's negotiating for the purchase of a software program for all his firm's accounts and records. Even if he educates himself on the basics of computer software, the salesperson on the other side of the deal will probably have an advantage because of her superior knowledge about the product.

This situation frequently arises with novice lawyers. Suppose you're negotiating with an experienced lawyer in a routine matter, such as a commercial real estate closing, and the other lawyer says, "This is the way lawyers in this area always handle escrow accounts for real estate taxes that will become due." You might have researched the law and spoken to other experienced lawyers and come to the conclusion that the other lawyer is wrong. But you still might have a nagging feeling that she knows what she's talking about. The other lawyer may have nothing more than psychological power over you because your inexperience makes you insecure. But unless you're willing to stand up to the other lawyer, that psychological power can be intimidating.

*The power to walk away.* Parties enter into a deal because they expect it to make them better off. If there's a better deal someplace else, a party should take that one, rather than the one being negotiated here and now. But if the party doesn't know about the better deal, the power to walk away is only dormant. To have that power and be able to use it, a party must develop a best alternative to agreeing to the deal on the table. The next section in this chapter explains why and how.

## §13.4 BEST ALTERNATIVE TO A NEGOTIATED AGREEMENT (BATNA)

A business person negotiating the business issues should know in advance exactly what her best alternative is if she fails to reach agreement with the other party. If she doesn't know that, she can't decide whether the agreement taking shape is in her own interests. If the deal being negotiated isn't better than her BATNA—better than any alternative deal she might reach elsewhere *and also* better than no deal at all—she should walk away. As William Ury explains:

> Your BATNA is your walkaway alternative. It's your best course of action for satisfying your interests without the other's agreement. If you're negotiating with your boss over a raise, your BATNA might be to find a job with another firm. If you're negotiating with a salesperson, your BATNA might be to talk to the store manager or, if that fails, you might go to another store. If one nation is negotiating with another over

unfair trade practices, its BATNA may be to appeal to the appropriate international tribunal . . . .[3]

If a drugstore chain wants to lease space in a building, for example, the building owner will wonder: "What other potential tenants might I lease the space to? Are there any alternative uses for the building? Are there any tax advantages to keeping the store vacant?" Each of these represents a potential alternative to signing an agreement with the drugstore chain: finding a different tenant, using the building in a way that does not involve leasing space or leaving the space empty for a time and taking a tax loss. The most profitable of them is the building owner's BATNA—the owner's best alternative to a negotiated agreement with the drugstore chain. If, during the negotiation, the BATNA turns out to be better than any possible deal with the drugstore chain, the building owner can walk away.

Business people intuitively think in BATNA terms, even if they've never heard of the concept. If a buyer doesn't know how much money other sellers would be willing to accept for the same type of asset, or if a borrower doesn't know the interest rate that other lenders would charge, that buyer or borrower will get taken advantage of in the market because of a limited understanding of comparison shopping. To thrive, a business person must continually develop alternatives to prospective deals.

For transactional lawyers, BATNA doesn't drive the contract negotiation in the same way that it does for business people. In the business negotiation, each party's BATNA is a dominant factor. But in the lawyer-to-lawyer contract negotiation that follows, it generally lurks in the background unless some issue pushes it back to being front and center. In negotiating the business deal, the business people must know what the alternatives are. When the lawyers begin their negotiations, the business people have already settled the conspicuous business issues where BATNA makes a difference. When the lawyers negotiate, their job is to memorialize that deal and, while doing so, to protect and advance the client's interests to the extent possible.

Suppose that in the course of the contract negotiation, you discover a risk that you cannot reduce through negotiation and that's bad enough that prudence requires a frank discussion with your client. You've discovered that the deal isn't what the client thought it was. The discussion between you and your client would naturally include some BATNA analysis. But that discussion is one you won't enjoy. The lawyer's job is to get the deal done by drafting a contract that implements the business agreement. Finding an issue that requires the client to think about BATNA raises the possibility of the deal failing while the lawyers are negotiating. Clients expect deal lawyers to use problem-solving skills to preserve the deal while protecting the client. But if that's impossible—truly impossible—a lawyer will have a BATNA discussion with a client, suggesting that the client decide whether to walk away. That would be a counseling discussion using the skills explained in Chapters 7 through 11.

---

3. William Ury, *Getting Past No: Negotiating Your Way from Confrontation to Cooperation* 21 (1993).

# CHAPTER 14

# PROBLEM-SOLVING AND POSITIONAL APPROACHES—COLLEGIAL AND COMBATIVE STYLES

## §14.1 PROBLEM-SOLVING VS. POSITIONAL NEGOTIATION

The two primary approaches to negotiation are problem-solving and positional. The problem-solving approach focuses on the parties' interests. The positional approach focuses on the parties' rights and power. Nearly all negotiations involve some degree of both approaches, but an explanation of the differences between them will help you make appropriate choices in selecting negotiation strategy and tactics.

Often a lawyer will use both types of approaches in the same negotiation. In preparing to negotiate, decide how much you'll problem-solve and how much you'll operate positionally. Most of what you do and say will depend on this decision.

If you assume that one approach is always preferable to the other, you'll be less effective than a lawyer who can function well using either approach.

## §14.2 THE PROBLEM-SOLVING APPROACH

In the problem-solving approach, two lawyers together engage in the process described in Chapter 3. This kind of negotiation emphasizes the *integration* of the resources each side brings to the table so that each party ends up better off. The problem-solving approach assumes that each side supplies something of value that can create benefits to both parties. During both of the two negotiations—by the parties on the business issues and by the lawyers on the legal issues—the negotiators try to integrate these interests into the final contract.

In transactional work, problem-solving negotiation occurs only when both sides recognize what Peter Siviglia, a New York deal lawyer, calls "the value of a fair agreement":

> When doing a deal, the parties and their attorneys must look for solutions. They must not turn problems into battle fields. And lest you think you can put something over on the other party, forget it. You can't. Absent one party's having an overwhelming bargaining position, such as a bank making a loan to a customer other than ExxonMobil, the contract will always be drawn into balance, hence, there is no shame in drafting a fair agreement. It's the right thing to do.[1]

A risk in problem-solving negotiation is that one of the lawyers might become seduced by a mood of collaboration and fail to get what the client needs. Your job is to reduce your client's risk, protect the opportunities your client obtained in the business issues negotiation, and in general put the client in a better position.

Even if the other lawyer will join you in problem-solving, that doesn't mean that the solutions you like will be agreeable to the other side. Finding solutions that work for both parties is hard work. Either lawyer might become frustrated with the other, and that frustration can cause the lawyers to start taking positions, which converts problem-solving negotiation into positional negotiation. To prevent that, build "a golden bridge"[2] between your client and the other party. The rest of this section explains how to do this.

*Keep focused on the parties' interests.* For problem-solving to work, the parties need to make their interests explicit and concentrate on developing solutions to meet these needs. If the parties become distracted and entangled in wrangles about rights and power, problem-solving will fail. If both lawyers work together to satisfy the parties' interests, problem-solving might succeed.

*Facilitate incorporation.* In a problem-solving negotiation, if each party presents its own proposal, the parties might become so entrenched in their advocacy that the bargaining can quickly become positional in nature. To avoid this problem, try to incorporate elements of the other party's proposal into the modification of your own client's proposal. By recognizing some reasonableness in the other party's proposal, you continue to acknowledge its interests and keep the door open to further problem-solving.

*Help the other party save face.* The reputational and psychological needs of the parties may be so important that any solution must address them. In such situations, think about ways to help the other party save face without compromising any of the priority interests of your own client.

---

1. Peter Siviglia, *Contracts and Negotiating for the Business Person: You and Your Lawyer* 45 (2006).
2. William Ury, *Getting Past No: Negotiating Your Way from Confrontation to Cooperation* 108 (1993).

## §14.3 THE POSITIONAL APPROACH

In positional negotiation, each party takes a position that she's entitled to something. Negotiation becomes a contest in which each party makes concessions, adopts fallback positions, and either eventually agrees to a compromise or leaves the bargaining table. Positional negotiators assume that bargaining is limited to the options available under common business practices or form contracts and agreements. Prevailing practices in the trade or business can become the "rights" about which the parties negotiate. The relative power imbalance between the parties can affect the ultimate distribution of the pot.

Many lawyers are naturally competitive people, and once they start taking positions, as Mnookin, Peppet, and Tulumello explain, negotiations over the legal issues

> can become highly adversarial. The parties may build one-sided demands into their initial drafts that they really don't care about but hope to concede away later as bargaining chips. On provisions that they do care about, each side may open with an extreme position and concede very slowly in hopes of wearing down the other side. The negotiation may become a game of chicken, where various terms are characterized as deal-breakers or "not subject to negotiation." Each side may try to create the impression that it has less to lose if the deal doesn't go through. Each may believe that the other side will blink first. Neither side learns much about the other's true interests or concerns, and creative trades to resolve their differences go unexplored. In the end, the lawyers may deadlock, with each side unwilling to back down and yet unsure just how far the other side can be pushed before they walk away from the deal. The clients may need to get involved—often to their annoyance—to get the deal moving again and save the transaction.[3]

In their well-known book on negotiation, *Getting to Yes*, Roger Fisher and William Ury reject positional bargaining:

> When negotiators bargain over positions, they tend to lock themselves into those positions. The more you clarify your position and defend it against attack, the more committed you become to it. The more you try to convince the other side of the impossibility of changing your opening position, the more difficult it becomes to do so. Your ego becomes identified with your position.[4]

A positional approach can make it difficult for your client to build or preserve a long-term relationship with the other party. But if the transaction is a one-shot deal with a party whom your client expects never to see again, there's no relationship to damage. You might still want to use a problem-solving approach, however, if you think it will produce a better agreement for your client.

---

[3]. Robert H. Mnookin, Scott R. Peppet & Andrew S. Tulumello, *Beyond Winning: Negotiating to Create Value in Deals and Disputes* 253–254 (2000).
[4]. Roger Fisher et al., *Getting to Yes: Negotiating Agreement Without Giving In* 4–5 (2d ed., 1991).

## §14.4 WHAT TO DO WHEN THE OTHER SIDE REFUSES TO PROBLEM-SOLVE

If the other lawyer is locked into positions, and if your client would be better off with problem-solving, try some of the techniques described in this section.

*Ask "Why?"* Try to get the other side to identify the interests underlying their position. Ask questions like these:

> Why is this important to your client?
> Could you help me understand your client's point of view?

You might be surprised at the answers. And the other lawyer might be surprised at your willingness to help protect her client's interests.

Everyone needs to feel heard and understood. That basic human need is rarely satisfied—especially in conversations between lawyers. When you truly hear and understand another person's point of view, it can profoundly influence their behavior.

*Ask "Why not?"* Some lawyers simply will refuse to answer a direct question about their clients' interests but may be eager to criticize your proposals. So after the other party's lawyer rejects your proposal, ask what's wrong with it, and the other lawyer might start talking about the interests that lawyer is expected to protect.

*Change the rhetoric.* You can influence the dynamic by asking questions like these:

> X might help both of us. It'll solve some of my client's problems. Would it help you in any way?
> Is there another way of handling this problem?

***Don't lecture the other lawyer about how and why to problem-solve.*** The other lawyer will feel condescended to. Your goal is to convince the other lawyer that such a problem-solving approach will in fact satisfy their interests better than positional bargaining. To accomplish this goal, get the other side talking about their interests, not just positional positions.

## §14.5 NEGOTIATING STYLES— COLLEGIAL AND COMBATIVE

In transactional work, combative lawyering can kill deals. Peter Siviglia explains:

> Commercial transactions are not—or at least they should not be—adversarial proceedings. Doubtless, there is an element of adversity because each party does have its own interests. Yet unlike litigation where the object is to win, the commercial transaction is not about winning; it is about doing a deal . . . that is, agreeing.

> Unfortunately, the focus of our legal system is combat. If there is any doubt, just turn on the television. Every program about lawyers is litigation oriented. . . . Confrontation makes for a good plot. Likewise, the training in law school . . . emphasizes litigation skills: debate, arguing a case, defending a point of view.
>
> An adversarial, argumentative approach is not conducive to concluding a deal. . . . [T]he objective of the commercial lawyer is not to defeat. Winning, in the commercial arena, is getting a deal done that makes sense to both parties. Coupled to this objective is a corollary: Get the deal done as efficiently and as smoothly as possible.
>
> So, whenever I start to write a contract or a term sheet for a transaction, I try the best I can to locate and understand the interests and concerns of the other party and to treat them in the document. The objective is to give the other party what is important to that party without hurting yourself.[5]

A combative style is tough, dominating, forceful, aggressive, and attacking. A collegial style is personable, friendly, and tactful. Obviously, there's a broad continuum between these two styles. And in any given negotiation, a lawyer might switch from one style to another, depending upon the impact the lawyer wants to make on the other side. Moreover, because style depends in large part on the perception of the listener, the precise attributes of a particular style will depend significantly on the culture in which the negotiation is taking place. That perception might vary from one region of the country to another, and it might vary from one type of law practice to another.

Don't try to become someone you aren't. How you negotiate will grow out of who you are. You can change your negotiation style or modify it to meet the needs of a particular situation, but to some extent, the way you negotiate will be determined by your personality.

In conducting any negotiation, select for yourself a style that will work well in the circumstances. Sometimes your selection will be based on the strategy you choose. If you're using a positional approach, you might select a combative style to demonstrate to the other party your client's confidence in her position. If you're using a problem-solving strategy, you might choose a collegial approach to encourage mutual brainstorming.

## §14.6 AN EXAMPLE OF STYLE

Laura was an associate at a commercial law firm.

> [O]ne day the senior lawyer she'd been working with went on vacation, leaving her in charge of an important negotiation. The client was a South American manufacturing company that was about to default on a bank loan and hoped to renegotiate its terms; a syndicate of bankers that owned the endangered loan sat on the other side of the negotiating table.
>
> Laura . . . nervously . . . took her spot in the lead chair, flanked by her client: general counsel on one side and senior financial officer on the other. These happened to be Laura's favorite clients: gracious and soft-spoken, very different from the master-of-the-universe types her firm usually represented. . . .

---

5. Siviglia, *supra* note 1, at 43.

. . . Across the table sat nine disgruntled investment bankers in tailored suits and expensive shoes, accompanied by their lawyer, a square-jawed woman with a hearty manner [who] launched into an impressive speech on how Laura's clients would be lucky simply to accept the bankers' terms. . . .

Everyone waited for Laura to reply, but she couldn't think of anything to say. So she just sat there. . . . Her clients shifting uneasily in their seats. . . .

[But she'd] prepared more than everyone else. She had a quiet but firm speaking style. She rarely spoke without thinking. Being mild-mannered, she could take strong, even aggressive, positions while coming across as perfectly reasonable. And she tended to ask questions—lots of them—and actually listen to the answers. . . .

"Let's go back a step. What are your numbers based on?" she asked.

"What if we structured the loan this way, do you think it might work?"

"That way?"

"Some other way?"

At first her questions were tentative. She picked up steam as she went along, posing them more forcefully and making it clear that she'd done her homework and wouldn't concede the facts. But she also stayed true to her own style, never raising her voice or losing her decorum. Every time the bankers made an assertion that seemed unbudgeable, Laura tried to be constructive. "Are you saying that's the only way to go? What if we took a different approach?"

Eventually her simple queries shifted the mood in the room. . . . The bankers stopped speechifying and dominance-posing, activities for which Laura felt hopelessly ill-equipped, and they started having an actual conversation.

More discussion. Still no agreement. One of the bankers revved up again, throwing his papers down and storming out of the room. Laura ignored this display. . . .

Finally the two sides struck a deal. . . .

[T]he next morning, the lead lawyer for the bankers—the vigorous woman with the strong jaw—called to offer her a job. "I've never seen anyone so nice and so tough at the same time," she said. And the day after that, the lead banker called Laura, asking if her law firm would represent his company in the future. "We need someone who can help us put deals together without letting ego get in the way," he said.[6]

---

6. Susan Cain, *Quiet* 7–9 (2012).

# CHAPTER 15

# NEGOTIATION DISCUSSIONS WITH THE OTHER PARTY'S LAWYER

## §15.1 TELEPHONE, EMAIL, LOCATION

On television and in movies, you're seen litigators negotiating face to face in law offices, in courthouse hallways, and outside judges' chambers. Although transactional lawyers do negotiate face to face, they also use email and the telephone extensively. In part, that's because transactional negotiation focuses on the written contract, drafts of which can be sent back and forth as email attachments.

But it's also because litigators and transactional lawyers deal with different clusters of issues. Face-to-face meetings facilitate agreement on big issues on which the entire agreement is based. In a transaction, that's often true of the business issues, which are settled by the clients before the lawyers are brought in to negotiate the legal issues. The legal issues are important, but they're often defined more specifically. There might be many of them, and they're often heavy with details. That lends itself to a series of phone conversations and emails.

In litigation, the two negotiations are merged into one. Litigators negotiate *everything*, including the litigation version of business issues—especially the money (how much the defendant will pay in exchange for the plaintiff's withdrawing the lawsuit) and delivery schedule (whether the money will be paid in a lump sum now or in installments in a structured settlement). Because litigators negotiate everything, they often need to meet face to face.

But for transactional lawyers, meeting face-to-face can be time-*in*efficient. Litigators are often in the same building—the courthouse—but transactional lawyers would have to travel to each others' offices. They'll avoid that if the issues can be handled effectively through other means.

***Telephone:*** A negotiation with many specifically detailed issues can often be done effectively through several phone conversations, especially when lawyers need to check facts and consult clients between phone calls. But body language doesn't travel through telephone lines, and subtle changes in voice tone sometimes aren't as apparent. Less rapport develops in non-face-to-face negotiations than during in-person meetings.

***Email:*** Email provides the flexibility to communicate at times convenient to the lawyers. And it's the fastest and most efficient way to transmit contract drafts, as attachments.

But more important, email provides an opportunity to plan carefully each response to what the other lawyer has said. Although many lawyers don't realize it, this opportunity to reflect is an enormous advantage—if you use it.

If you don't take time to reflect and plan carefully, your emails risk becoming flammable. Your initial feeling on reading the other lawyer's email messages can be frustration. When you quickly write and send a response, your frustration can seem accusatory to the lawyer who reads that response. Often people writing emails don't have the same inhibitions they'd have in face-to-face meetings or over the telephone.

You might fail to temper your frustration because you can't see the other lawyer in front of you or even hear the other lawyer's voice. Sometimes you're actually having a dialog with your keyboard and computer screen—not with another human being. The other lawyer might be doing the same thing. She can't hear nuances, inflection, and human connection in your voice. She can only read disembodied words with none of the context that even voice communication over the telephone provides. When misunderstandings occur, they are usually negative.

In addition, many students use an informal email style that's inappropriate to serious negotiations especially when precise wording of an agreement is at issue. Everywhere in legal work, an appearance of professionalism gives you credibility. An inappropriately informal style in email can jeopardize that credibility.

You'll use email continually because of its efficiencies in communicating at any time of day and in transmitting drafts. How can you take advantage of its benefits without incurring its risks?

Use the opportunity to reflect. Draft an email and store it in your "Drafts" box, which most email systems provide. A few hours later, read it and rewrite it. In all forms of writing—office memos, appellate briefs, and contracts—first drafts are wretched. Good writing is really good *re*writing, which you learned in your first-year legal writing course. That's still true in contract drafting—and it's also true in email writing. Reread and rewrite. Reread again and rewrite again. Then send.

Combine email with other, more personal means of communications. Don't conduct extended email exchanges. Recognize the point when human discussion would be productive. Then use the telephone to brainstorm. Problem-solving is often impossible by email. It requires human discussion.

Occasional small talk by telephone has another advantage. Think of it as rapport maintenance. When email exchanges start to seem cold, use the telephone to develop or redevelop the relationship between the lawyers as two human beings trying to get the parties' deal to work. And if you need to make negative comments, do it in a phone conversation rather than email.

In email specify what you're agreeing to or not agreeing to. And say exactly what you'd like the other lawyer to do. Move the negotiation along. Unless you're doing nothing more than sending attachments, emails are often action communications.

Remember that email is easily forwarded by the recipient to others. Don't write anything in an email that you wouldn't want lots of other people to read—including your client, the other party, any lawyer who supervises you, online blogs, and judges and juries. If the parties later sue each other, your emails may be discoverable.

Sometimes present your arguments in a formally drafted attachment rather than in the message itself. When the precise wording of an agreement is at issue, this method will especially help you carefully prepare your argument. Email messages should be short. Anything not short should be an attachment.

*Location for face-to-face meetings:* An advantage to hosting the negotiation is that you can have the resources you need under your command—your files, research materials, and support staff. You feel more in control of the situation. But there are also advantages to negotiating on the other party's turf. You can demonstrate your intent to cooperate by consenting to meet at the other lawyer's office. And when you're away from your own office, you can honestly excuse yourself if you do not have the necessary materials on hand.

## §15.2 PLANNING THE ISSUES AGENDA

*Prioritizing:* List all the issues you need resolved, as well as those the other party will probably raise. Then prioritize. Decide which issues matter most. Peter Siviglia suggests that lawyers

> focus . . . on the important issues; and generally there are only a few of these. . . . The inexperienced negotiator tends to treat all points with equal importance and has difficulty making decisions. . . . Good negotiators determine from the outset what issues are important to their side and what issues are important to the other side. They then try to obtain as much as they can of those which are crucial to them and try to accommodate the other side as much as possible.[1]

You want to obtain as much as possible on the issues you consider most important for your client, while compromising more readily on those at the bottom of your priorities.

Now consider the sequence in which you'll address these issues. Initial consideration of minor issues can be effective if you want to establish a collegial relationship with the other party that facilitates the negotiation of more difficult issues. This approach can help if you're using problem-solving methods in the

---

1. Peter Siviglia, *Commercial Agreements: A Lawyer's Guide to Drafting and Negotiating* 363 (1993).

negotiation and are concerned about the other party's willingness to engage in such bargaining.

But starting with the small issues delays the inevitable negotiation over the major ones. Sometimes that's a disadvantage. If the big issues are resolved in your favor early, you know how much you can afford to compromise on the smaller ones. And if you don't get what you want on bigger issues, you can revisit them later and trade on smaller issues in exchange for revisiting the bigger issues and renegotiating them.

*Overlawyering:* A good deal lawyer knows when enough is enough.

It's time for a deal lawyer to stop when she has thoughts like this: "We could spend a lot of time ironing out the wording on issue X so that my client's interests are protected. And we could run up several hundred dollars or thousands of dollars in lawyers' fees to do that. On the other hand, this issue stands only a very small chance of blowing up or will cause only minor dislocations if it does."

When lawyers *don't* know when to stop, they overlawyer and kill deals (see §2.6). Mnookin, Peppet, and Tulumello explain:

> Over-lawyering . . . can waste the client's time and money by focusing on small or unlikely risks that do not justify contractual planning. For example, during a merger negotiation, James Freund—then-partner in the New York law firm of Skadden, Arps—was asked by the other side to negotiate a set of clauses that would take effect in the unlikely event that the 1933 Securities Act was repealed. . . . The critical consideration to keep in mind is whether the net expected impact of the risk justifies the cost (in both money and relationships) required to allocate it before the fact.[2]

But don't compromise on a client's true interests. Know *exactly* when enough is enough.

## §15.3 REQUESTS, DEMANDS, OFFERS, AND CONCESSIONS

*Requests and demands.* You know what a request is. A demand is a request delivered in an aggressive, inflexible, and positional manner implying that the only acceptable answer is yes. Demands narrow the conversation. Requests keep open the possibilities for better solutions.

Suppose you've demanded X, and the other side has said no. Because you presented it as a demand, the other lawyer could reasonably have inferred that you weren't open to brainstorming the subject. Suppose you had instead requested X. The other lawyer might have said, "I can't do that, but we might be able to do Y instead." You might have jumped for joy because Y is so much better for your client than X, and you hadn't realized until then that Y was possible. The other lawyer might also have offered Y in response to your demand—but she is much more likely to do it if you ask nicely.

---

2. Robert H. Mnookin, Scott R. Peppet & Andrew S. Tulumello, *Beyond Winning: Negotiating to Create Value in Deals and Disputes* 148 (2000).

It's not a sign of weakness to ask nicely—as long as you do it firmly. For example, you can use collegial words with a tone of voice that conveys confidence that your concerns deserve respect. Both clients want the deal to go forward, and the lawyers are supposed to help that happen. Many transactional lawyers speak in a refreshingly civilized way, although the phrasing will differ regionally and depending on the lawyer's practice specialty. For example,

> My client needs comfort on matter X.

Here's the translation:

> My client is at risk because of X. I want some way of reducing or eliminating that risk. I might be thinking about some contract conditions or maybe having your client represent and warrant in the contract something about X. I'm open to discussion. Let's talk.

*Offers and concessions:* When you make an offer, you propose an exchange. For example, you'll agree to the other lawyer's force majeure clause if the other lawyer agrees to your anti-assignment clause. The trading isn't usually that blunt, however. And you might want some details changed as part of the trade:

> I think I might be able to live with your force majeure clause, although I'd feel better if labor slowdowns weren't covered. It can be hard to tell the difference between a slowdown and an inefficiency not caused by a labor union. Is my anti-assignment clause acceptable to you?

This doesn't sound like a trade, but it is. The lawyer has offered a concession (accepting the other lawyer's force majeure clause, with a small modification) and then immediately mentions the possibility of a counter-concession (the other lawyer's agreeing to the anti-assignment clause). And the offered concession isn't to the entire force majeure clause. The lawyer offering that concession wants labor slowdowns deleted before she agrees. She offers a good, objective reason. Providing that reason together with the wording—"I might be able to live with," "I'd feel better if," "acceptable to you"—obscures what's really happening. Here's the translation:

> I'll agree to your force majeure clause if you take out labor slowdowns and agree to my anti-assignment clause.

In some practice specialties, lawyers say exactly that. In others, it seems crass, and lawyers there would say something like the longer version above. Perhaps the most jarring thing about the shorter version is the omission of an objective reason for taking out labor slowdowns.

In the longer version, the lawyer might be worried that including labor slowdowns could create a risk for her client. She can say that, and then the lawyers could talk about how to allocate that risk. Instead, she states an objective reason—that including labor slowdowns is impractical—which sidesteps an argument about which party should be at risk. The objective reason helps both lawyers feel that they're producing an objectively fair contract. But even if the lawyer had stated her true reason—limiting her client's risk—the other lawyer should be able to respond constructively.

Regardless of how it's expressed, what's happening is horse trading facilitated by log-rolling. Horse-trading is an exchange, one concession for another. Logrolling is offering concessions to create momentum toward agreement. (Horses and logs aren't involved. These are just figures of speech used by some but not all lawyers.) When a lawyer offers concessions, she may expect that the other lawyer will owe some counter-concessions later in return. If the other lawyer never makes those counter-concessions, the first lawyer may have to say,

> I agreed to X, Y, and Z earlier. I hope your client can be accommodating on the issues I'm raising now.

The way you communicate the offer is crucial to its effectiveness. The keys to such a presentation are *credibility* (you're serious about this and have thought it through carefully) and *justification* (you're providing reasons, whether objective or subjective, that the other side can accept). Sound reasons make it easier for the other lawyer to agree to give you what you want even if she doesn't agree with your reason.

When you make a concession, think about how to package it that will minimize an impression of weakness. You don't want to look like you give away concessions easily. Rapid, and especially large, concessions send the opposite message. And if you make a series of concessions without receiving any from the other side, you communicate only a weak commitment to your client's needs.

Give the other lawyer a reason for every concession you make. Otherwise, it will seem to the other lawyer you give away concessions for free. If you force yourself to give a specific justification for each concession, you impose a self-discipline that helps you resist the psychological pressure many novice lawyers feel to make concessions just to "get along" with the other side. If you can't identify a rationale for a concession, you probably shouldn't make it.

When lawyers engage in positional rather than problem-solving negotiation, the discussions can harden, as Mnookin, Peppet, and Tulumello explain:

> Each side may start with an initial draft agreement that is highly partisan in its favor. The prototype is the landlord's lease—a standard form that is extremely skewed in favor of the landlord. Then each lawyer may try to wear the other side down so that the other side will grant valuable concessions on various terms. This is not entirely irrational, of course. As in any negotiation, each side faces great strategic uncertainty and neither party wants to be overly generous initially for fear of giving away more than is necessary to do the deal. Each side may thus dig in to an initial position that claims most of the value of the deal and fight hard to concede little while demanding concessions from the other side. If one party seems to be in the more dominant or powerful position—perhaps because it has greater resources or has better alternative in the marketplace—it may demand that the deal be structured on its terms and refuse to negotiate over those terms with the weaker party.
>
> When a lawyer says "There can be no deal unless you provide a warranty in the form I've suggested," this creates a basic problem. Is it really true? Or is the lawyer trying to create the perception that the provision is indispensable when it isn't? The lawyer may be playing a game of chicken just to see how important this provision is to you and whether you're willing to risk having the deal blow up over it.

The result may be deadlock. If the lawyers on both sides stake out extreme positions on legal terms, they may argue back and forth without moving the deal forward. Eventually, one or both clients may intervene to get the deal done—particularly if they get impatient with their lawyers for delaying the negotiations.[3]

If the clients have to intervene to get the deal done, at least one of these lawyers, and maybe both, can be seen as deal killers by the clients. To a client, a deal-killing lawyer creates problems rather than solves them.

Some clients, however, deliberately hire lawyers who look like deal killers but actually aren't. If the client usually has the stronger market position because it's large and powerful and other parties to its deals are typically small and weak, that client might hire hard-nosed lawyers to exploit the client's more powerful position.

*Anchors and first offers:* Anchoring most often happens with numbers, which the parties are concerned with in the business issues negotiation. But lawyers sometimes negotiate numbers. And anchoring can happen with concepts, such as the substance of a contract provision. And it often happens with contract wording, which matters a great deal when you decide whether to draft language or let the other lawyer draft it (§15.4).

How we perceive a particular offer's value is influenced by numbers, concepts, and contract language that enter the negotiation environment through that offer. These numbers, concepts, and contract language anchor the discussion by providing a context for everything that follows on that topic. First offers thus can have anchoring effects. Even when lawyers and business people know they shouldn't let themselves be influenced that way, they often succumb to an anchor's influence.

For example, when you walk into a new car showroom, the first offer has already been made. It's on the window of every car in the showroom. It's called the sticker price. The dealer doesn't expect you to accept that offer. It's an artificial number, and its sole purpose is to create an anchor. The dealer wants the rest of the negotiation to be a question of how much less than the sticker price you'll pay. Most new car buyers succumb to the anchor and negotiate down from the sticker price. This is always a mistake.

The most effective way of handling the other side's anchor is to ignore it. In the new car dealer's showroom, don't even look at the sticker, and if a salesperson brings it up, refuse to talk about it. Instead, create your own anchor by making the real first offer yourself.

Find out how much the dealer paid to buy the car wholesale. (*Consumer Reports* and other sources will provide that information for a small fee.) Add enough money to cover the dealer's overhead and provide a reasonable profit. Reduce the total somewhat to give yourself negotiating room. Then offer to buy the car for the number you calculated this way. You and the dealer will then haggle based on your anchor, and you'll probably pay a price a little higher than your first offer. You have to let them win some concession from you. You reduced your number so you could make that concession.

---

3. *Id.* at 147–148.

You destroyed the dealer's anchor by ignoring the sticker price—pretending that the dealer has not made the first offer—and by insisting that the number you put on the table is the true first offer and establishes the real anchor.

The same process should inform how you handle drafting contract language. The next section in this chapter explains why.

## §15.4 WHO DRAFTS

In the end, what matters are the *exact words* in the contract. Lawyers certainly haggle over the concepts—what the conditions are, what's being represented and warranted, and so on—but the words used in the contract to express the concepts determine what the concepts actually are. If the parties later want to know exactly what they can do and must do, the words control. If the parties later dispute, in resolving that dispute, the words control.

Too often a lawyer pays more attention to a concept than to the words that will express that concept in the contract. In so doing, the lawyer cedes some power to the other lawyer if the other law takes the initiative and drafts. Whoever initially chooses the words has the power to anchor them for the reasons explained in §15.3.

The lawyer who drafts isn't free to change green into blue. But the drafting can specify, within limits, something about the *shade* of green—and thus anchor that shade. The nondrafting lawyer must then (1) notice that the shade favors the drafter *and* (2) take on the burden of negotiating for a different shade. Many nondrafting lawyers do neither, or they do the first but not the second. And to negotiate for a different shade, the nondrafting lawyer might need to trade for it by making a concession elsewhere in the contract. That's the effect of words that anchor.

A lawyer has other reasons as well for doing as much of the drafting as possible. Peter Siviglia explains them:

> The task of drafting [the contract] requires the draftsman to acquire a comprehensive understanding of the entire deal. From the beginning, that person will understand, better than anyone else, the transaction both on macro and micro level. With that knowledge, there is less likelihood of overlooking something, some provision, some treatment, that should be part of the contract. . . .
>
> It is also safer, much safer, to be the draftsman for another reason. With so few exceptions that I can almost use the word "invariably," the initial draft of any contract will be changed. And amending an agreement is a tricky assignment. In fact, I would rather write an agreement from scratch then amend one, because . . . a change to one part of the document often requires conforming changes elsewhere; and that possibility requires an examination of the entire contract as well as any related documents. Knowledge of the entirety of the transaction, coupled with a detailed knowledge of the contract, will minimize the risk of oversight.[4]

---

4. Peter Siviglia, *Contracts and Negotiating for the Business Person: You and Your Lawyer* 47 (2006).

## §15.5 INFORMATION BARGAINING

In negotiation, each party needs to learn more information from the other because information is itself power in bargaining. To prepare, identify (1) information you want to obtain from the other party so you can understand its bargaining stance; (2) information you want to disclose voluntarily to the other party to facilitate your overall plan; and (3) information you want to conceal that might weaken your negotiation posture.

*Obtaining information:* Ask. You'll get much more information by listening and questioning (§§4.1–4.3) than you will by making arguments (§4.7) and other kinds of statements. "Statements generate resistance, whereas questions generate answers."[5] If questions and listening aren't producing information, consider using silence. "If you have asked an honest question to which they have provided an insufficient answer, just wait. People tend to feel uncomfortable with silence, particularly if they have doubts about the merits of something they have said."[6]

Verify what you think you know, and negotiate over what you don't know. Section 12.2 and Appendix E explain why and how.

*Disclosing and concealing information:* Sometimes lawyers want to give complete information precisely. And sometimes they would rather not.

In problem-solving negotiations, you'll want to explain details about your client's interests so you and the other lawyer can collaboratively work to satisfy those interests. But even then, you might not want to tell the other lawyer everything.

Suppose your client spent over ten years building a business from something that started in his garage into an enterprise that employs 1,000 people and has revenues of $200 million a year. He's now selling the business, and during negotiation, the buyer's lawyer asks what your client plans to do after the sale. If you want to provide a lot of information, you could say:

> He enjoys building up a company from nothing. That's his thrill. And the only business he knows is manufacturing the product he's making now. He's had a few ideas in the last two years for revolutionary changes in the product that would make everything now on the market obsolete. But he hasn't developed them through this company because he knew he was going to sell it and start over. He's already talked informally with investment bankers to get a new company up and running. He's written a business plan already, and the bankers are eager to lend the money, although nothing will be agreed to until after he has taken six months off to travel around the world.

This is interesting. In other situations, it would be exactly the right thing to say. But in this negotiation it tells the other lawyer so much that her client might walk away from this deal to avoid your client's new company.

If you want to give the *smallest* amount of information possible, you could answer by speaking incompletely, ambiguously, or both:

---

5. Roger Fisher et al., *Getting to Yes: Negotiating Agreement Without Giving In* 111 (2d ed. 1991).
6. *Id.* at 112.

He's explored some business ideas, but nothing is certain yet except that he and his family will take a trip around the world for the next six months. They'll go to Paris, Prague, Kenya—the sort of places where you can relax and get away from an exhausting business life. He was telling me the other day about plans to visit the Studio Ghibli museum in Japan. He's an entrepreneur by nature. He'll get into one of his ideas when he gets back.

Here, the details about the trip are a smokescreen. This ambiguous, incomplete answer contains no untruthful statements. If the buyer's lawyer wants to know whether the seller will compete in the same market, she needs to ask that question directly and listen carefully to the answer. (The ethical rules governing an answer like this one are explored in §16.1.)

Two kinds of skills are involved here. The first is knowing *when* to speak completely and precisely and *when* to speak incompletely or ambiguously. The second is knowing *how* to speak in those ways.

# CHAPTER 16

# SOME COMMON PROBLEMS IN NEGOTIATION

## §16.1 ETHICAL ISSUES IN NEGOTIATION

*False statements.* It's unethical for a lawyer to "knowingly make a false statement of material fact or law to a third person"[1] or help a client to do so. If the false statement is about a fact (rather than about the law), it's a misrepresentation. Not only is a knowing misrepresentation punishable under ethics law, but it also exposes the lawyer and the client to tort liability if the other party relies on it and suffers as a result.

A knowing misrepresentation (a concept of ethics law) is also typically an intentional misrepresentation (a tort also known as fraudulent misrepresentation or fraud). Under the doctrine of respondeat superior, the lawyer's actions are imputed to the client because the lawyer is the client's agent. Even if the misrepresentation is accidental, a misrepresentation can lead to rescission of the contract. Thus, the client can lose all the benefits of the contract if the misrepresentation induced the other party to deal. Appendix E explains the contract consequences of misrepresentation.

"Puffing," however, isn't misrepresentation. That's because it's not a statement of fact. A statement is puffing if, in the context, the other side typically would treat it as background noise rather than an assertion of literal truth. If a car salesperson tells you that the vehicle you're looking at is "fun to drive" or "you'll love it," that's puffing. You would not treat these as statements of hard fact. But if the salesperson tells you that the car has done well in government crash tests, gets 43 miles per gallon on the highway, and accelerates from zero to 60 miles per

---

1. Rule 4.1(a) of the ABA Model Rules of Professional Conduct.

hour in less than seven seconds, those are representations, and if they're not true, they're misrepresentations.

"Under generally accepted conventions in negotiation," according to the Model Rules of Professional Conduct, "certain types of statements ordinarily are not taken as statements of material fact."[2] Thus, "my client will never agree to that" is puffing because it will ordinarily be heard as posturing and rhetoric. A statement of fact might be "my client sent me an email yesterday instructing me to reject that." If the client sent no such email, the lawyer has misrepresented.

Ethical problems can also occur when you omit mentioning a fact. Under the Model Rules, a "lawyer shall not knowingly . . . fail to disclose a material fact to a third party when disclosure is necessary to avoid assisting a criminal or fraudulent act by a client, unless disclosure is prohibited by Rule 1.6."[3] With narrow exceptions, Rule 1.6 prohibits a lawyer from revealing "information relating to representation of a client unless the client gives informed consent [or] the disclosure is impliedly authorized in order to carry out the representation . . . ."[4] Generally, under these rules, a lawyer is not obligated to disclose information that will harm her client's negotiating position. Indeed, a lawyer who discloses confidential information without the client's consent commits an ethical violation.

*Scriveners' errors.* A lawyer is ethically required to correct a scrivener's error even if the client objects and even if the other party's lawyer hasn't noticed it. A *scrivener's error* is an inaccurate expression in a written contract of what the parties have agreed to. A *scrivener* is literally a person who writes down what she's told to write down, and a scrivener's error occurs when a scrivener is told one thing and writes down another. In a contract, a lawyer acts in part as a scrivener. If the parties or their lawyers have agreed on a provision, the scrivener part of a lawyer's job is to draft that agreement accurately into the contract.

A written contract is not the actual contract. The actual contract is the meeting of the minds between the parties—what they agreed upon. The written contract is *evidence* of that. If every copy of a written contract is accidentally destroyed in a fire, that does not free the parties of their contractual obligations. The fire only makes it harder to prove what those obligations are.

The simplest kind of scrivener's error can occur when the parties agreed on one number, perhaps the price, and another number appears in the contract. Even in a standard-form, preprinted contract with blanks to be filled in, the wrong number might have been written into one of the blanks. In a lawyer-to-lawyer negotiated contract—where the parties negotiated the business terms and the lawyers negotiated the legal terms and memorialized everything in a written contract—a scrivener's error also can include inaccurate expression of the lawyers' agreements on legal issues:

> A simple example might occur in a contract for sale, where the price of the commodity is, say $4,300 but is written $3,400. Another, not unusual occurrence is dropping a word. For example: "You will be responsible for our expenses" as opposed to "You will *not* be responsible for our expenses." or sometimes the mind, perhaps in haste or

---

2. Comment 2 to Model Rule 4.1.
3. Model Rule 4.1(b).
4. Model Rule 1.6(a).

exhaustion, loses the train of thought and uses the wrong word, as in "You will pay the travel expenses" instead of "*We* will pay the travel expenses."[5]

If a scrivener's error hurts one of the parties later, that party will likely notice the difference between what the parties agreed to and what the contract says they agreed to. And if that party can prove a scrivener's error (the difference between the agreement and the written contract) through clear and convincing evidence, a court will reform the contract to express the agreement accurately.[6] Because of the remedy of reformation and because parties and their lawyers often remember or have kept written notes about what they agreed to before signing the written contract, only rarely does a scrivener's error actually hurt one party and benefit the other. That rare situation happens only where the hurt party can't remember what it agreed to, or it can't produce clear and convincing evidence that the contract inaccurately expresses the agreement, or the cost and uncertainty of litigation outweigh the harm. Clients sometimes think that a scrivener's error in their favor is a lucky windfall, but it isn't.

Because the written contract is evidence of the actual contract, a lawyer has the following ethical duties where she notices a scrivener's error in the client's favor *before* the written contract is executed by the parties:[7] The lawyer must correct the error by redrafting the inaccurate wording, either unilaterally or in collaboration with the lawyer on the other side of the deal. She has no obligation to tell the client of the error or that it's being corrected. She is ethically required to correct it even over the client's objection and even if the other side hasn't noticed the error. If she permits the parties to execute a contract that she knows inaccurately expresses their agreement, she may be participating in fraud.

But if the lawyer notices the error only *after* the parties have executed the contract, the lawyer's duties are less clear. A lawyer is not obligated to tell another party that that party has a cause of action against the lawyer's own client. If a client is sued by the other party seeking rescission, the lawyer can ethically defend the lawsuit by insisting that the plaintiff carry its burden of proof. In a reformation lawsuit, the burden in most states is clear and convincing evidence, which is harder for a plaintiff to satisfy than the usual civil standard of preponderance of the evidence.

## §16.2 THREATS AND WARNINGS

A *threat* is a statement of intent to assert a right or power if the other party doesn't comply with a request or demand. It's an attempt to use rights or power to coerce the other side to agree. When a lawyer or party has been threatened, the response is typically to make a counter-threat. That's because the initial threat is often felt as an insult, an attack on the dignity of the person threatened. After the

---

5. Peter Siviglia, *Contracts and Negotiating for the Business Person: You and Your Lawyer* 46 (2006).
6. *Benyon Bldg. Corp. v. Nat'l Guardian Life Ins. Co.*, 455 N.Y.2d 246 (Ill. App. Ct.).
7. ABA Informal Opinion 86-1518 (1986). See *Stare v. Tate*, 98 Cal. Rptr. 264 (Cal. App. 2d Dist. 1971).

counter-threat, both parties have been insulted. Often threats make it harder for the parties to agree and certainly much harder to form a continuing relationship.

Fisher and Ury say that "threats are one of the most abused tactics in negotiation."[8] In many circumstances, threats aren't tactics at all. They're a distraction.

In litigation, lawyers can get so wrapped up in pointless threats that they talk past each other rather than with each other. Each lawyer brags about the quality of her evidence ("we have three witnesses who say your client ran the red light") and the likelihood of prevailing at trial ("the jury will be upset about my client's injuries") while demeaning the other lawyer's evidence ("nobody's going to believe your pathologist") and the other party's chances at trial ("I think you're going to lose"). This goes on like a barroom argument, each lawyer trying to top the other and each getting annoyed at the other, until finally both realize that time is running out, trial will start shortly, and their clients prefer a deal. Then, without much thought about why, the lawyers quickly come to an agreement that's about halfway between the positions they started with. This isn't really negotiation at all. It's a prolonged threat display, followed by a quick splitting of the difference. Neither side has really influenced the other, and neither has thought about the issues enough to plan a careful negotiation. Threats aren't a substitute for brainstorming and other forms of problem-solving.

Deal lawyers don't have a BATNA (§13.4) similar to a litigator's option to try the case. Deal clients expect their lawyers to produce a contract. But sometimes you'll need to do something *instead of* a threat.

***Give warnings rather than threats.*** Sometimes logical arguments and attempted problem-solving have no effect, the other party refuses to make concessions your client absolutely needs, and the other party refuses to discuss alternative solutions. If your client has rights or powers that can make the other party feel insecure enough to behave differently, you may want to use that leverage.

Surrendering to a threat humiliates the threatened person. Your goal is to make the other lawyer feel insecure but also respected. Insecurity can motivate the other lawyer to change behavior. Respect can help the other lawyer do that without losing dignity. People will do what you want not because you force them to, but instead because you persuade them to do it and make it easier for them to do it. Effective negotiators master the art of *warning*.

To determine whether you have leverage on which a warning can be based, compare your client's rights and power with the other party's. Imagine what counter-warnings the other lawyer might make in response to yours. Ask yourself what impact a warning from you would have on the negotiation.

Think of ways of packaging the warning in the form of observations and suggestions that demonstrate the existence of the right or power without drama. "A threat comes across as what *you will do* to them if they do not agree. A warning comes across as *what will happen* if agreement is not reached."[9]

---

8. Roger Fisher et al., *Getting to Yes: Negotiating Agreement Without Giving In* 136 (2d ed. 1991).
9. William Ury, *Getting Past No: Negotiating Your Way from Confrontation to Cooperation* 137 (1993).

> *Threat*     If you don't agree to give my client X, Y, and Z, we'll walk, and this deal will die because my client will buy from somebody else.

You can't threaten that. Your client expects you to produce a contract—not destroy the deal.

> *Warning*    Without X, Y, and Z, the deal looks very different from the way it looked to my client when the parties were negotiating the price my client would pay. The legal issues, as we're discussing them, seem to be raising the risks high enough that a buyer in my client's position might naturally think about whether it might be better to buy elsewhere [*that's the warning*]. I don't want my client to think that because I want this deal to work [*a clarification that this is a warning and not a threat*], but I'm beginning to worry about it. Could you and I find a way to prevent it so that both of our clients get what they need [*an attempt to convert positional bargaining into problem-solving*]?

Warnings work only if they're credible and will have a significant impact on the other party. If they lack credibility, the other party will just laugh them off. Peter Siviglia says,

> Never bluff. If you bluff and get caught, you lose credibility. And once credibility is lost, the other party will not take you seriously and will probably be able to push you further on other points than had you not been caught in the bluff. For example, several times in negotiations, the other side threatened to leave. I was taking a hard line on important points and I had the leverage. I said: "You know where the door is; no one is stopping you." They never did leave. And the rest was a piece of cake.[10]

***Responding to threats and warnings.*** When you're confronted with a threat or warning, you have some options.

You can ignore it if you believe that the other party's claimed right or power is weak or that the other party won't carry it out. If your client won't be significantly affected even if the threat or warning is carried out, you can explain why it'll have little impact and then continue the bargaining.

Or you can make a counter-warning of your own. A counter-warning, however, can lead to an escalation of tensions and a breakdown in bargaining. You may want to try to soften your presentation of the counter-warning: "My client does know several suppliers who can sell the same goods in volume. But let's not be distracted by other buyers and sellers and get back to the terms of this deal."

---

10. Siviglia, *supra* note 5, at 363.

# APPENDICES

# APPENDIX A

# TYPES OF CONTRACTS

Contracts with closings are fundamentally different from those without closings.

## CONTRACTS WITH CLOSINGS

A closing is a meeting at which the core transactions of a deal are accomplished. During the closing, both parties perform. For example, a buyer pays money to a seller and the seller transfers ownership to the buyer.

*Asset sales:* A closing is usually necessary in the sale of a substantial asset. The bigger the asset, the more likely that one or both parties will insist on simultaneous deliveries of title and purchase money. The terms *purchase* and *sale* are not synonymous. To sell is to deliver title and receive the purchase money. To buy is to deliver the money and receive title. Neither can happen without the other, but they're different acts and separate duties.

Picture the seller handing a deed to the buyer while the buyer hands money to the seller. It's rarely that simple, however. In complicated deals involving millions of dollars, the closing can last for hours. Hundreds of pages of documents might be involved. And the money might be delivered by electronic interbank transfer coordinated by telephone from the room where the closing occurs. Certainly the sale of a factory or a ship would need a closing, but so do transfers of less expensive assets.

Every house sale involves a closing. Even car sales involve closings. In all these situations, the seller will not surrender the asset before being paid, and the buyer will not pay before receiving the asset. The solution is for the parties to perform simultaneously.

*Financing agreements (loans) involving a security interest:* A closing allows the lender to take a security interest in property owned by the borrower simultaneously with releasing the loaned money to the borrower. At the closing, the lender will deliver the money, and the borrower will sign a lien-creating document and probably a promissory note. A home mortgage is a common example of a loan where the lender takes a security interest in an asset (the home) and a closing would usually be needed.

*Closings in general:* At a closing, more may be needed than delivering money, title, and security-creating documents. If a third party would be affected or would need to be satisfied, documents affecting the third party might need to be executed. For example, if an asset buyer will insure the asset, the insurer may require evidence of the transfer as well as the condition and value of the asset. If a government regulatory agency cares about the transaction, documents satisfying the agency may need to be executed. If a party is a corporation, documents required for a corporate act may be needed.

Sometimes two closings will happen at the same time. Most residential real estate closings are really two simultaneous closings on two separate contracts. The buyer is a party to both contracts. In the purchase contract, the other party is the seller. If the buyer pays with borrowed money (as most buyers do), the other party is a lending bank, and a mortgage loan closing happens at the same time as the purchase closing. For the purchase contract, the seller delivers title and the buyer pays for it. For the loan contract, the buyer (who's also a borrower) signs a promissory note and a document giving the lending bank a mortgage lien. The bank delivers the loan money, which the buyer uses on the spot to pay part of the purchase price to the seller. The closings are simultaneous because the bank wants a lien on the house at the same instant it delivers the money to the buyer. The buyer can't create that lien without title. And the seller won't deliver title without being paid. The buyer and seller might not understand all this. But the real estate agent and the lending bank understand it perfectly.

Closings can happen even if one of the parties hasn't realized it. If you buy a new car from a dealer, you'll sign a purchase contract and come back a few days later to pick up the car and pay for it with a certified check or a bank check. When you come back, the dealership will deliver title and you will deliver the money. That's a closing, even if nobody at the dealership called it that. You contracted to buy, and the dealer contracted to sell. At the closing, you'll both perform on your promises. You'll execute documents that will satisfy a regulatory agency (your state's department of motor vehicles). The dealer will produce documents you'll need to satisfy a third party (your insurer). And if the dealer arranged your financing, the loan closing will happen at the same time. The dealership isn't lending you money. It will be acting as an agent for a lending bank. You might not understand that this is a closing, or two closings. But it is.

## ■ CONTRACTS WITHOUT CLOSINGS

Most deals don't involve a closing. Here are some examples: a revolving credit contract (like the one you have with your credit card company); a licensing contract (like the one you clicked through without reading when you downloaded iTunes into your computer); and a services contract (like the one you signed when you opened up a bank account and the bank agreed to perform the service of storing your money).

*Purchase agreements where a closing is impractical or unnecessary:* For example, an auto manufacturer contracts with a supplier to deliver 5,000 seat belts per business day to the auto manufacturer's assembly lines, which are located in factories in several cities. A closing is impractical because so many deliveries are involved. Another example: you order something from a website that charges your credit card before you receive the goods. Neither party wants the inconvenience of a closing. And you're willing to run the risk of foregoing a closing because usually the item arrives in good condition, and if it doesn't, the seller is usually willing to fix the problem.

*Debt agreements (many but not all):* A closing is unnecessary where the loan will not be secured (example: a student loan) and impractical where both parties want the debt transacted quickly or more than once (example: credit card debt).

*Service agreements:* A closing is impossible where the service will be provided in the future. Examples: a lawyer retainer agreement, an insurance policy.

*Licensing agreements and intellectual property transfer agreements:* License contracts are usually worded so that the license is created instantly when the parties execute the contract. An example: Disney/Pixar licenses McDonald's to give away character toys from Disney/Pixar movies.

# APPENDIX B

# DOCUMENT DESIGN FOR CONTRACTS

## PAGE LAYOUT

*Justification:* Justification determines where lines of type begin on the left side of the page and where they end on the right side. Left-justified text starts exactly at the left margin, and each line ends wherever its last word would naturally end. The left side of the text (its left margin) is a straight vertical line, but its right side (its right margin) looks ragged when your eye scans it from the top of the page to the bottom. But if text is fully justified, both margins are vertically straight. This page is fully justified.

The default setting on your word processor is probably left-justification. That's fine. If your default is full-justification, you should change it to left-justification, at least when you draft contracts. In computer-generated documents left-justified text is easier to read.

*White space:* Too much type on a page can make it difficult and unpleasant to read. Creating white space opens up the page and makes it less crowded and easier on the eye.

Your word processor's default margins are probably 1 inch on each side. You can create white space by moving the left and right margins each a quarter inch toward the center of the page, so they become 1.25 inches.

You can also create white space by the way you handle headings. In a single-spaced document, many drafters will skip a line above a heading and skip another line below it. Instead, skip two lines above the heading. That would make your organization more visually obvious. The heading would more clearly belong to the text below it because twice as much white space would appear above. If your document is double-spaced, you can get similar results by hitting the Enter key twice above the heading and once below it.

*Section layout:* Indent the first line, as though it's the first line of a paragraph. Tabulate subsections and subdivisions of subsections like the following:

> Section 42. Force Majeure. xxxxxxxxxxxxxxxxxxxxxxxxx xxxxxxxxxxxxxxxxxxxxxxxxxxxxxxxxxxxxxxxxxxxxxxxxxxx xxxx
>
> > (a) xxxxxxxxxxxxxxxxxxxxxxxxxxxxxxxxxxxxxxxx xxxxxxxxxxxxxxxxxxxxxxxxxxxxxx
> >
> > > (i) xxxxxxxxxxxxxxxxxxxxxxxxxxxxxxxxxxx xxxxxxxxxxxxxxx

Enclose the letter or number completely in parentheses: "(a)"—not "a)".

A subsection is a subdivision of a section. The minimum number of subsections is two. If you've written a section with only one subsection, you haven't accurately subdivided the section.

## FONTS AND TYPE SIZE

A font is a group of letters and numbers with a common design. Type size is how big the letters and numbers are, usually measured in points.

*Bold type:* Put the following in bold type: the contract title at the top of the first page, the contract title in the first line of the preamble, the recitals or background heading (if you use a heading there), article headings (if the contract is divided into articles), and the section number and the caption (section title) that follows the section number at the beginning of each section.

*Default settings:* Your word processor is probably Microsoft Word or Corel WordPerfect. Your word processor's default settings are probably 12 point (type size) and either Times New Roman or Calibri (fonts), which look like this:

Times New Roman
Calibri

Your word processor will produce one of these automatically unless you or someone else has changed your default settings.

*Adjusting type size:* Near the top of your Word or WordPerfect screen is a little window that tells you which font the word processor is using. Next to it is an even smaller window that tells you the size of the type (a number). In Word 2007 and Word 2010, those windows are on the top left. In earlier versions of Word, they're to the right of the top center of your screen. In WordPerfect, they're on the top left.

Each of those windows will open a drop-down menu that lets you change the font or the type size. The menu opens if you click on a little down-arrow next to the window. Depending on the font, you'll use either 11 point or 12 point. Choose a point size that's large enough to be read easily, but not so large that a page holds too little text.

In a contract, an article heading should be one point larger than the text. The contract title at the top of the first page should be two or three points larger than the text.

*Choosing a font:* First, decide whether to use a serif font or a sans serif font. A serif font has little lines (serifs) at the edges of letters. A sans serif font doesn't have those lines. (*Sans* means "without" in French.) Look at the two fonts illustrated earlier in this appendix. Times New Roman has serifs. Calibri does not.

Serifs help your eye move quickly through dense text, which is why they're used in books.

Sans serif fonts are more readable when words that will be glanced at (headings, signs, advertisements). Sans serif fonts are also good for words that will be studied carefully, one or two sentences at a time.

Most lawyer-drafted contracts come out of computer printers in serif fonts. That's because lawyers are creatures of habit, not because serif fonts are inherently better for contracts. A contract isn't read like a book, page after page, from beginning to end. Typically, the reader glances through the contract to find a particular provision and then studies the few sentences in that provision. Those two things—glancing and studying—are helped by a sans serif font because a page without serifs looks uncluttered as you try to find a relevant provision and then read its few sentences carefully.

Don't use a sans serif font in a dense-text document like an office memo or appellate brief. Serifs help the reader's eye move through dense, paragraphed text. It's possible to use a sans serif font in a contract only because tabulation produces white space not found in dense, paragraphed documents. (And you should be tabulating in the contracts you draft.)

Regardless of the type of document, the font you choose ought to

1. look professional,
2. be easy to read, and
3. please the eye.

If you want to experiment, take something you've already written, change its font, and see how it looks. If you're not happy with the result, change it again until you find a font you like.

Print out a sample page in the font you're considering. You don't need to print the whole document. A sample page is enough. But make the decision based on a printed page—not on how the font looks on a computer screen. Many fonts that look good on the screen don't look as good when printed. And most readers will read the contract on paper, not on a screen.

To change a document's font in Word, you may need to block the entire document and click on a font in the drop-down menu. In WordPerfect, just put the cursor at the beginning of the document and click on a font from the drop-down menu.

If you find a font you want to use all the time, you can change your word processor's font default. Search the word processor's help function for how.

Windows computers have all the fonts illustrated below. Apple computers have many but not all of them. An Apple font not illustrated here might work as well as these.

*Sans serif fonts:* Below are some sans serif fonts that look professional, are easy to read, and are pleasing to the eye:

    Calibri
    Candara
    Corbel
    **Twentieth Century MT**

*Serif fonts:* Although a well-chosen sans serif font can make a contract somewhat more readable, it's not wrong to use a good serif font in a contract—if you choose the serif font carefully. Here are some serif fonts that look professional, are easy to read, and are pleasing to the eye. (Times New Roman is included for comparison only.)

    Book Antiqua
    Century
    Century Schoolbook
    Constantia
    Goudy OlSt BT
    Goudy Old Style
    Palatino Linotype
    Times New Roman

Document design specialists say that Times New Roman is harder to read than the other fonts shown here. The Supreme Court refuses to accept briefs in Times New Roman. The Court instead requires that briefs be submitted in a font in the Century family. For that reason, Century and Century Schoolbook are common substitutes among lawyers for Times New Roman.

Constantia almost always looks professionally readable. It may be the most versatile serif font shown here.

Book Antiqua and Palatino are similar except that Palatino has more space between the lines.

The two Goudys are closely related but are not identical. Goudy OlSt BT is more spacious than Goudy Old Style.

# APPENDIX C

# SOME CONTRACT DRAFTING CONSIDERATIONS

This appendix is not a substitute for a drafting textbook. It's only a reminder of some recurring problems that are more fully explained in a drafting textbook.

## ■ COVENANTS

A *covenant* is a promise to do or not to do something. Lawyers use the words *covenant*, *duty*, and *obligation* to mean the same thing.

Covenants are not the solution to all problems—or even most of them. When parties agree that one of them is supposed to do X, that does not mean that you should automatically create a covenant. Sometimes what they've agreed to is really a condition. If the consequence of not doing X should be damages, create a covenant ("shall"). If the consequence would be that something else in the contract is activated, create a condition ("if X"). (See Appendix D.) If the consequences should be both, create both a covenant and a promissory condition. (Again, see Appendix D.)

The fundamental difference between a covenant and a condition is the consequences. If a party fails to perform a covenant, the consequence is damages. If a party fails to satisfy a condition, that party doesn't get something it wants (whatever the condition is attached to). A condition can be attached to a covenant, discretionary authority, a declaration, or (rarely) a warranty. Representations cannot be conditioned. (See Appendix D.)

In most but not all situations, you can create a duty by doing this:

1. Make the party who has the duty the subject of the sentence.
2. Add the word "shall" or the words "shall not" (depending on whether the party is obligated to do something or to refrain from doing it).

3. After "shall" or "shall not" state exactly what that party is supposed to do or not do.
4. If the duty is conditioned, add the condition or conditions at the beginning or end of the sentence.

In a standard-form consumer contract, use "must" instead of "shall." Consumers can understand "must" but might not understand "shall."

Don't use the word "shall" for any other purpose. Lawyers throw the word "shall" all over contracts and create ambiguity when they do it. Courts have to waste the parties' money figuring out whether "shall" sentences express covenants, discretionary authority, declarations or conditions. If you use "shall" only to create covenants, your contracts will be much clearer.

When you create a duty, do it precisely and completely. Wherever you impose a duty, be specific enough that the parties will know exactly what conduct equals performance and exactly where breach would begin. Who has the duty, and what *exactly* is that person supposed to do? With most covenants, specify time, place, manner of performance, etc.

Imagine that you're the party with the duty; you intend to do everything expected of you; and you really want to know—*exactly*—what to do. You want clear instructions so you can obey them. Read each of your covenants in that frame of mind, asking yourself things like "What exactly does that party have to do to avoid being in breach?" If the covenant you've written doesn't answer that question, redraft it.

If time matters, set a precise deadline ("by noon on July 10" or "no later than the first day of each month").

What is the standard of performance? What quality of work is good enough? Be specific. See §12.2.

## DISCRETIONARY AUTHORITY

Discretionary authority is the power (but not the obligation) to do something. Discretionary authority and power mean the same thing.

In most situations, you can create discretionary authority by doing this:

1. Make the party with the power the subject of the sentence.
2. Add the word "may."
3. After "may" state exactly what that party has the power to do.
4. If the power is conditioned, add the condition or conditions at the beginning or end of the sentence.

## DRAFTING GENERALLY

Specify standards. Wherever the quality of something could vary, provide a standard. If the standard can be objective and specific, draft it that way. Many standards must be subjective, however, because there's no practical way to formulate them objectively. See §12.2.

In a definition, don't describe. Define. A definition lists the characteristics that make the thing being defined different from everything else. The following is not a definition: "North America is a continent in the western hemisphere." Those words merely describe. They don't specify what makes North America unique—different from everything else. The western hemisphere includes two continents, and the descriptive words could apply to either of them. Here's a real definition: "North America is the land mass that extends from the Panama-Colombia border to the Arctic Ocean." Only one thing on earth meets that definition.

Use cross-references where needed for clarity. Where one part of the contract refers to something provided for in another part, use a specific cross-reference: "If the Buyer fails to do X as required by section 32.3, the Seller may do Y."

Don't provide the same thing twice. It creates risk of inconsistency, which could create ambiguity. Do it once and completely. If you need to bring the matter up twice, make one of those instances a cross-reference to the other.

Don't leave gaps. "If sales exceed $500,000 in the first month, royalties are those set out in Schedule 4.12. If sales are less than $500,000 in the first month, the Licensor may terminate." What if sales are exactly $500,000? What happens then?

Don't double-state numbers. This is distracting clutter: "within ten (10) business days." Lawyers do it out of fear of making a mistake when digits turn out to be wrong. But it just doubles the chance of making a mistake (twice instead of once), which is easy to do when the number is big. Either way, a mistake creates ambiguity. Double-stating numbers can't prevent this problem. Only careful proofreading can prevent it.

# APPENDIX D

# CONTRACT CONDITIONS

Conditions are essential to contract design. They're controls that make the deal work. They can activate or deactivate covenants, discretionary authority, and declarations—turning them on or off. They can link covenants so that performance of one party's duty to do X requires the other party to do Y. And they're ways of managing risk, so that one party, for example, doesn't have to perform unless the other party is performing.

A condition is something that must be satisfied to activate or deactivate something else in the contract. The "something else" could be a covenant, discretionary authority, or a declaration. In each of these examples, the "if" clause is the condition.

*covenant:* If the tenant fails to pay the rent by 5:00 P.M. on the day it is due, the tenant shall pay a penalty of $25 per day until the rent is paid.

*discretionary authority:* If the tenant fails to pay the rent for two consecutive months, the landlord may terminate this lease.

*declaration:* If the premises are destroyed, this lease terminates as of the date of destruction.

*Every* condition has *all* three of the following characteristics:

*characteristic #1* how the condition was created

*characteristic #2* how it relates to time

*characteristic #3* how it activates the covenant, discretionary authority, or declaration that it conditions.

For example, the covenant example above includes an express (characteristic #1) condition precedent (characteristic #2) that operates as a promissory condition to a covenant (characteristic #3). The covenant example has all three of these characteristics.

The rest of this appendix explains the characteristics.

### Characteristic #1
### How the Condition Was Created

Every condition is either express or constructive.

*Express conditions* are stated as conditions in the contract's wording. All the examples at the beginning of this appendix are express conditions. Robert Lloyd calls express conditions "the real tools of the working lawyer":

> Express conditions are what the lawyer uses to control the way the deal progresses. They're what she uses to make sure her client is protected every step along the way ... all the legal doctrine surrounding express conditions is pretty straightforward. That's why express conditions are such a useful tool—they're so reliable.[1]

Never let a condition you want in the contract go unexpressed. Otherwise, your client might have the gruesome task of trying to persuade a court to find an unexpressed, constructive condition.

*Constructive conditions* are *not* expressed as conditions in the words of the contract. If the parties litigate, a court would have to decide whether the logic of their agreement implies a condition that has not been expressed in the written contract. A constructive condition issue is a horrible thing to litigate. The parties will fight over whether a condition exists. And they'll fight over what exactly the condition might be. The fighting will be expensive, and it's unpredictable how a court will rule.

If you want something *not* to be conditioned and if you're concerned that the other side might later argue that there's a constructive condition, insert into the contract a declaration that no condition exists ("The Borrower's obligation to make timely payments is unconditional").

### Characteristic #2
### The Condition's Relationship to Time

Every condition is precedent, concurrent, or subsequent.

*Conditions precedent:*   The duty arises when the condition is satisfied.

    *example:*   If the buyer's engineer approves the structure, the buyer shall deliver a deposit of ten percent of the purchase price.

---

1. Robert M. Lloyd, *Making Contracts Relevant*, 36 Ariz. St. L.J. 257, 275–276 (2004).

*Conditions subsequent:* The duty exists *unless* the condition is satisfied.

> *example:* The buyer shall deliver a deposit of ten percent of the purchase price unless the buyer's engineer disapproves the structure.

The only real difference between a condition precedent and a condition subsequent is who has the burden of proof. *The party who wants the condition to have been satisfied must prove that it was.* A condition precedent activates an otherwise dormant duty. A condition subsequent deactivates (makes dormant) a duty that had been active.

Suppose the thing conditioned is a borrower's covenant. If the condition is precedent and the borrower breaches, the lender, in a suit for damages, must prove the condition was satisfied. That's because the lender wants to prove breach, and a dormant duty can't be breached.

But if the condition were subsequent, the borrower would have the burden of proof. The borrower's duty was active—and could have been breached—until the condition is satisfied.

Drafters don't bother to think about this when they draft conditions—but they should think about it. If you want the other party to have a burden of proof in case of a dispute, choose the type of condition that would accomplish that, and then draft accordingly. To create a condition precedent, draft an "if" clause. To create a condition subsequent, draft an "unless" or "except" clause. If you're concerned that a court might misconstrue what you're doing, be more specific ("It is a condition precedent to the Borrower's obligation to do X that Y has occurred").

If the other party has drafted a condition precedent where you would rather have a condition subsequent—or vice versa—insist that it be changed. If the other side is consciously trying to assign a burden of proof to your client, you might need to negotiate that.

*Concurrent conditions:* Mutual duties are to be performed simultaneously. One party's tender of performance is a condition of the other party's duty to perform.

> *example:* The buyer shall deliver the remainder of the purchase price, and the seller shall convey title.

In a contract with a closing (see Appendix A), each party's *tender* of performance at the closing is a condition to the other party's duty to perform. Tendering is offering to perform. In a house sale, for example, the buyer tenders by bringing the money (in the form of a bank check) to the closing, and the seller tenders by bringing the deed. If the buyer arrives without the money, the seller has no obligation to put the deed in the buyer's hands. If the seller arrives without the deed, the buyer has no obligation to put the money in the seller's hands.

These concurrent conditions don't need to be spelled out so specifically in the contract. If the contract requires a closing, the concurrent conditions are expressed by the requirement to close. Thousands of closings happen every day and every transactional lawyer and every judge knows how closings work.

### Characteristic #3
### How the Condition Activates the Covenant, Discretionary Authority, or Declaration

The examples below illustrate the relationship between a condition and a covenant, but conditioned discretionary authority and declarations work the same way.

**Pure conditions:** Satisfying the condition is not within either party's control.

> *example:* If the property suffers weather damage before the closing, the seller shall repair the damage.
>
> *the condition:* If the property suffers weather damage before the closing, . . .
>
> *the covenant:* The seller shall repair the damage.

Neither party can influence the weather.

**Promissory conditions:** This is a two-fer. One party's promise to perform (a covenant) is also a condition to one of the other party's covenants. "A shall do X. If A does X, B shall do Y." Expressing a promissory condition badly in a contract can create ambiguity, and ambiguity can lead to litigation. This one is clearly and unambiguously expressed:

> *example:* The seller shall remove all liens on the property. If the seller removes all liens, the buyer shall purchase the property.
>
> *covenant:* The seller shall remove all liens on the property.
>
> *condition to another covenant:* If the seller removes all liens, . . .
>
> *the other covenant:* The buyer shall purchase the property.

**Discretionary conditions:** This is the discretionary equivalent of a promissory condition. A party may fulfill the condition but is not required to. If the party does satisfy the condition, the duty is activated.

> *example:* The seller may terminate this contract. If the seller terminates the contract, she shall refund the buyer's deposit.
>
> *discretionary authority:* The seller may terminate this contract.
>
> *condition to a covenant:* If the seller terminates the contract, . . .
>
> *the covenant:* She shall refund the buyer's deposit.

# APPENDIX E

# MANAGING THE RISK OF THE UNKNOWN: DUE DILIGENCE, REPRESENTATIONS, AND WARRANTIES

Representations and warranties[1] are among the tools used in a contract to manage and allocate risk—specifically, the risk of the unknown. In virtually every deal, one party or both will make factual assumptions. If one of those assumptions turns out not to be true, the value of the deal can change for the party that has made the assumption.

When you buy a Toshiba laptop, for example, you're assuming that it's really a Toshiba and not a fake by an unknown manufacturer; that the parts you can't see, such as the processor and hard drive, really do have the characteristics claimed in an advertisement; that the seller actually owns or will own the laptop and can transfer its title to you; and that the laptop will work for a reasonable time after you buy it. If any of these assumptions turns out not to be true, the laptop is worth less to you than you thought it would be.

Buyers worry about whether what they're buying is good enough. Sellers worry about whether the buyer will pay.

*Due diligence:* One way of managing risk is to perform due diligence by investigating. For example, the laptop seller performs due diligence by getting authorization from your credit card company before letting you have what you're buying.

---

[1]. See Tina L. Stark, *Drafting Contracts: How and Why Lawyers Do What They Do* 11–19, 113–119 (2007).

Some forms of due diligence involve issues that lawyers can't help investigate, such as the odds involved in market risk. Markets fluctuate with supply and demand. Suppose your client is buying a ten-year supply of aviation fuel or some other form of petroleum, locking in the current market price for the entire term of the contract. If the market price rises continually over those ten years, your client will be in petroleum heaven, and the seller will be in petroleum hell, because your client will be paying below-market prices for years. But if the market price falls continually over that time, the parties' situations will be reversed. The parties might deliberately incur all this risk, each betting on future market prices. Or they might agree to reduce each party's risk by negotiating automatic price adjustments to mitigate extreme market fluctuations. But these are business decisions based on business predictions.

Lawyers enhance due diligence in other ways. If a buyer is contracting to purchase the Bar-Z cattle ranch, the buyer's lawyer should negotiate for provisions permitting the buyer's experts to inspect the assets thoroughly before the deal closes, together with conditions on the buyer's obligation to purchase based on the results of that inspection. For example, the buyer would want to have an accountant examine the ranch's business records to see whether it's as profitable as the buyer hopes. If the buyer's obligation to close will be conditioned on the results of the inspection, the seller's lawyer should be negotiating for provisions to assure that the inspection will be accurate. The seller's lawyer should insist, for example, that the livestock be inspected by a large-animal veterinarian with cattle experience. The seller's lawyer should be worried about an inspection done by a veterinarian whose practice involves primarily dogs, cats, and other household pets.

*Representations and warranties:* Representations and warranties are a substantial part of deal negotiations between lawyers. Each lawyer tries to reduce her client's risk by getting the other party to make representations and warranties.

A party is better protected if it gets both a representation and a warranty for each material fact that the other party knows or could know firsthand. A prudent lawyer reduces risk *both* through due diligence *and* by obtaining representations and warranties. The rest of this appendix explains why and how representations and warranties are valuable.

*Warranties:* Every promise in a contract is either a warranty or a covenant. A *covenant* is a promise of action (for example, that the website selling the laptop will deliver it to you) or nonaction (the website won't charge your credit card before it ships the laptop to you). A *warranty* is a promise of a fact (such as that the seller owns the laptop you're buying or that it'll work for a year after you buy it).

When a promise is broken, it has been *breached*. A covenant is breached if the website doesn't deliver the laptop to you or if it charges your credit card before shipping the laptop to you. A warranty is breached if the website selling the laptop doesn't own it or if the laptop stops working a week after you bought it.

*Representations:* A representation is a statement of fact made by one party to the other to induce the other party to deal. It's *not* a promise. It's a statement intended to induce reliance. Because it's not a promise, it can't be breached. A representation that turns out to be untrue is a *misrepresentation*. A misrepresentation is a tort in a contract setting.

Through a warranty, a party can promise a past fact (the laptop was manufactured by Toshiba), a present fact (the seller owns it now), or a future fact (it'll work for a year). But only past and present facts can be represented. The law of torts doesn't care about the future. A seller can represent and warrant both that Toshiba manufactured the laptop and that the seller owns it now. A statement that the laptop will work for the next year can be a warranty but not a representation.

*Remedies:* Because a warranty is a promise, the remedies for breach are similar to those for breach of a covenant. They're the damages you studied in the first-year Contracts course. Misrepresentation remedies are more complex and differ greatly from state to state. But the basics are explained in the next few paragraphs.

A misrepresentation can often be a ground for avoidance, which relieves a party from a contract's obligations. That party can sue for rescission of the contract. Or, if the party is a defendant who's been sued for contract breach, the misrepresentation can be used as a defense to the plaintiff's claim. In both situations, the party suffering from the misrepresentation avoids the obligation to perform.

A party that avoids a contract, might also get restitution. Restitution is a contract law remedy that restores to one party a benefit wrongly obtained by the other party. For example, if a buyer has paid some of the purchase price, and if a court later rescinds the contract, the buyer can typically get the payment back through restitution.

To get damages, however, the party suffering from the misrepresentation must make a choice. A court will not award both avoidance (perhaps with restitution) *and* damages for harm caused by the misrepresentation. The aggrieved party must choose between avoidance and damages.

Because misrepresentation is a tort committed in a contract setting, damages might be tort compensatory damages, contract damages, or some blend of the two. The Restatement (Second) of Torts and the Restatement (Second) of Contracts are not perfectly consistent with each other on this point. States differ on how they compute misrepresentation damages, and the differences are so complex that explaining them is beyond the scope of this book. Availability of damages can also depend on whether the misrepresentation was innocent, negligent, or intentional (see the discussion of burdens of proof below). In many states, damages are available only if the misrepresentation was intentional.

When negotiating and drafting the contract, you can't possibly know whether any of the other party's representations will turn out to be misrepresentations— much less whether a misrepresentation might be innocent, negligent, or intentional. And you can't predict whether, if the deal breaks down in some future year, a client would be better off with contract damages for warranty breach or with whatever remedies might be available for misrepresentation.

Any attempt to predict wouldn't be more than a guess. To preserve flexibility for the future, a prudent lawyer therefore obtains from the other party both a representation and a warranty for each material fact that the other party knows or could know firsthand.

*Burdens of proof:* Breach of a warranty is almost always easier to prove than misrepresentation, as the diagram below shows. This is another reason to get a warranty with every representation. If you can't prove misrepresentation later, you might still be able to prove breach of warranty.

Because a misrepresentation is a tort, its elements include state-of-mind concepts, such as intent to induce reliance and intent to defraud. But a party's state of mind is irrelevant to breach of a promise, in this case breach of a warranty. In contract law, it doesn't matter whether a breach was accidental or deliberate. The only thing that matters is whether the nonbreaching party got what it was promised.

States generally recognize a distinction between intentional misrepresentation and less reprehensible forms. The diagram shows a typical state's burdens of proof. It might or might not be accurate for the state whose law will govern your client's claims.

### Cause of Action Elements for Misrepresentation and Breach of Warranty

|    | innocent misrepresentation | negligent misrepresentation | intentional misrepresentation | breach of warranty |
|----|---------------------------|----------------------------|------------------------------|--------------------|
| 1. | a statement of fact | a statement of fact | a statement of fact | a promise that |
| 2. | intended to induce reliance | intended to induce reliance | intended to induce reliance | a statement of fact is true |
| 3. | plaintiff relied | plaintiff relied | plaintiff relied | the statement is not true |
| 4. | reliance justifiable | reliance justifiable | reliance justifiable | |
| 5. | statement was material to the deal | statement was material to the deal | statement was material to the deal | |
| 6. | statement was not true when made | statement was not true when made | statement was not true when made | |
| 7. | (no state of mind element—strict liability) | defendant made the statement negligently | defendant made the statement with intent to defraud | |

For the three forms of misrepresentation, elements one through six are identical. They differ only in the seventh element—the defendant's state of mind at the moment she misrepresented.

Breach of a warranty is easier to prove because it has only the three elements shown in the diagram. And breach of warranty doesn't include the misrepresentation elements that are hardest to prove—states of mind such as the defendant's intent to defraud (intentional misrepresentation) or the defendant's negligence (negligent misrepresentation).

You can't predict today what kind of evidence your client will have years later. It often turns out that a plaintiff can prove breach of a warranty—but not misrepresentation. Even if at some future date misrepresentation remedies look better than warranty breach remedies, that difference will be worthless if your client can't prove all the misrepresentation elements. You won't always be able to get what you want in a future dispute, but if you've negotiated and drafted the contract carefully to provide alternatives, you might still be able to get what you need.[2]

---

2. Rolling Stones, "You Can't Always Get What You Want" (1969) ("You can't always get what you want/But if you try sometimes, well you just might find/You get what you need").

# INDEX

*(References are to section numbers.)*

Active Listening, 4.2
Advice, see Counseling and Advice
Amy, Jake, Inclusive Solution, 3.5
Arguments, making, 4.7
Assumptions, see also Due Diligence, Representations and Warranties
    by client, 6.7
    professionalism and, 2.3

Best Alternative to a Negotiated Agreement (BATNA), 13.4
Bovis General Contractors, 7.4
Business Issues and Legal Issues, 1.4, 12.1

Clients, generally, Chapter 5
    client as colleague and collaborator, 5.2
    client-centered lawyering, 5.1
    decisions by client, 5.3
    goals and preferences, 9.1
    like and dislike in a lawyer, 5.4
    working with transactional clients, 5.5
Client Interviewing, generally, Chapter 6
    assumptions by client, 6.7
    fee agreement with client, 6.9
    long-conversation, 6.1, 6.3–6.9
    short-conversation, 6.1–6.2
    "supposed-to," agreed to by parties, 6.7 (see also Conditions and Covenants)
    questions, 6.7–6.8
    what to ask about, 6.7
Closings, Appendix A
Cognitive Illusions, 11.4–11.5
Communications Skills, see Oral Communications Skills
Conditions, see also Covenants
    drafting, Appendix D
    negotiating, 12.2
    "supposed-to," agreed to by parties, 6.7
Convergent and Divergent thinking, 3.3
Counseling, generally Chapters 7–11
    advice, 7.1, 8.1
    client goals and preferences, 9.1
    clients who exclude lawyers from important decisions, 7.4
    client's stated goal might not be what client wants, 11.2
    cognitive illusions, 11.4–11.5
    conversation with client, Chapter 10
    counseling, examples of, 8.2–8.3
    decision, asking client to make, 10.5
    ethical issues in, 11.1
    meeting with client, Chapter 10
    moral dimension, 11.1
    options, developing and structuring so client can decide, Chapter 9
    plant closing example, 8.3
    predicting what each option would cause, 9.3
    preparing for, Chapter 9
    recommendation by lawyer, client's request for, 10.4
    risk, client's tolerance for, 9.4
    solutions, developing, Chapter 9
    unwise decision by client, 11.3
Covenants, see also Conditions
    drafting, Appendix C
    "supposed-to," agreed to by parties, 6.7
    negotiating, 12.2

Deal Stages and Dispute Stages, 1.3
Discretionary Authority, drafting, Appendix C
Document Design, Appendix B
"Deal-Killers" (lawyers who sabotage their clients' deals), see Overlawyering
Diagnosis, Chapter 3
Divergent and Convergent Thinking, 3.3
Drafting, 15.4, Appendix C
Due Diligence,
    assumptions by client, 6.7
    managing risk, Appendix E

Ebola, 7.4
Efficiency, professionalism, 2.4
Empathy, communicating, 4.4
Ethics,
    counseling, 11.1
    decision-making, lawyer and client, 5.3
    negotiation, 16.1

Fonts, Appendix B
Fraud, see Representations and Warranties

Gilligan, Carol, 3.5

Inclusive solution, 3.5
Integrity, professionalism, 2.1
Interviewing, see Client Interviewing

Jake, Amy, Inclusive Solution, 3.5
Judgment, excellent 2.1

Legal Issues and Business Issues, 1.4
Listening, 4.1–4.2

Negotiation,
    anchors, 15.3
    best alternative to a negotiated agreement (BATNA), 13.4
    business issues and legal issues, 1.4, 12.1
    client, working with during negotiation, 12.5
    collegial and combative, 14.5–14.6
    concessions, 15.3
    demands, 15.3
    email, 15.1
    endgame provisions, negotiating, 12.2
    ethical issues in, 16.1
    general provisions, 12.2
    information bargaining, 15.5
    interests, each party's, 13.1
    labels, negotiating, 12.3
    offers, 15.3
    planning issues agenda, 15.2
    positional approach, 14.3
    power, each party's, 13.3
    preparing to negotiate, 12.4, 15.2
    problem solving approach, 14.1–14.2, 14.4
    puffing, 16.1
    representations and warranties, negotiating, 12.2, 16.1, App. E
    requests, 15.3
    rights, each party's, 13.2
    scrivener's errors, 16.1
    standards, negotiating 12.2
    styles, collegial and combative, 14.5–14.6
    "Supposed-To" (whether a covenant or a condition), negotiating, 12.2
    telephone, email, location, 15.1
    threats, 16.2
    warnings, 16.2
    who drafts, 15.4
Numbers, professionalism, 2.5

Options,
    problem-solving, Chapter 3
    counseling, Chapter 9
Oral Communications Skills, generally, 2.4, Chapter 5
    active listening, 4.2
    arguments, making, 4.7
    asking questions, 4.3
    body language, 4.6
    empathy, communicating, 4.4
    listening, 4.1–4.2
    painting a picture, 4.5
    tone of voice, body language, 4.6
Overlawyering, generally, 2.6
    clients who exclude lawyers from important decisions, 7.4
    in counseling, 7.4
    in negotiation, 15.2

Painting a Picture, 4.5
Prediction,
    counseling, in, 9.3
    problem-solving, Chapter 3
Problem-Prevention, see Problem-Solving
Problem-Solving, generally, Chapter 3
    counseling, Chapter 9
    creativity, 3.2–3.3
    diagnosis, Chapter 3
    divergent and convergent thinking, 3.3
    Gilligan, Carol 3.5
    inclusive solution, 3.5
    prediction, Chapter 3
    process of, 3.2
    professionalism, 2.2
    strategy, Chapter 3
    style, 3.4
Professional Responsibility, see Ethics
Professionalism, generally, Chapter 2
    assumptions, 2.3

balanced life, 2.7
efficiency, 2.4
goals, 2.2
integrity, 2.1
judgment, 2.1
numbers, 2.5
overlawyering and underlawyering, 2.6
problem-solving, 2.2
taxes, 2.5

Questions, generally, 4.3
client interviews, 6.7–6.8
information bargaining, 15.5
negotiation, when the other side refuses to problem-solve, 14.4

Representations and Warranties, see also Due Diligence
assumptions by client, 6.7
ethical issues, 11.1, 16.1
managing risk, Appendix E
negotiating, 12.2

Scrivener's Errors, 16.1
Solutions, see Problem-Solving
Standards, 12.2
"Supposed-To" (whether a covenant or a condition), see also Covenants and Conditions
agreed to by parties, 6.7
negotiating, 12.2
Strategic Thinking, Chapter 3

Taxes, 2.5

Underlawyering, 2.6

Warranties, see Representations and Warranties